Lacan and Chan Buddhist Thought

Lacan and Chan Buddhist Thought provides a close reading of how Lacan mobilizes concepts from Chan Buddhist philosophy, culture, and practice in his later teachings.

The book emerged from the three co-authors' engagement with Lacan's 1962–1963 Seminar on Anxiety, and the significance of Lacan's original interpretation of the Buddhist principle that desire is the cause of suffering. The book reads key Lacanian concepts – such as the *objet a*, jouissance, the real, Nirvana, and the mirror – through ancient Buddhist teachings and koans. With this focused exploration of psychoanalysis and Chan Buddhism, the authors offer a philosophically grounded cross-cultural approach to the theory and practice of psychoanalysis in Asian countries.

Lacan and Chan Buddhist Thought will be a rich resource for psychoanalysts, academics, and students interested in Lacan and religion, the intellectual and cultural relationship between Asian and Western thought, and Mahayana Buddhism more generally.

Raul Moncayo, PhD, is a supervising analyst and past founding member and former president of the Lacanian School of Psychoanalysis, USA. He is the author of seven books on Lacanian psychoanalysis. Together with Yang Yu and Hong Zhou, he founded the Beijing Center for Freudian and Lacanian Psychoanalysis and Research to transmit a Lacanian psychoanalysis with an ongoing, active engagement with Chinese culture. In 2019, he founded the Blue Mountain Zen Center of El Cerrito, California.

Yang Yu is Associate Professor of English Literature at Beijing Normal University, candidate analyst of the Bay Area Lacanian School of Psychoanalysis, and founding member of the Beijing Center for Freudian and Lacanian Psychoanalysis and Research. She has published several journal papers on Lacan and English literature.

"This book is one of the clearest and most interesting introductions to Lacan. Since Chinese people are familiar with Buddhist thought, interpreting Lacan from this perspective makes the reader feel especially at home and helps to understand some of Lacan's extremely difficult concepts. This book is very suitable for Chinese readers to study Lacan and the writers present Lacan with such depth and lightness that the reader will find it a pleasure to read. The interpretation of the name *Lackhan* is very helpful in understanding the two otherness inside and outside the subject, and the explication of the concepts of jouissance, pleasure, and the Real is very illuminative and greatly clarify their complexities. In the works published in China on Lacan, there are only a few references to the relationship between Lacan's thought and Buddhism which are not so systematic. Therefore, this book, and eventually a Chinese translation, will have a great academic impact that will not only help to popularize Lacanian theory in China but will also orient a new trend in studying Lacan."

– **Xiaoyi Zhou**, *Peking University,*
Professor Zhou earned his doctorate at
Lancaster University in 1993 and has published widely
on comparative literature and literary theory

"What a treat to read this profound, careful, and creative exploration of Lacan and Chan Buddhism. East-West illuminate and add to each other, amplifying Lacan's vocabulary and concepts and Chan's existential evocations. Although Bion was not part of this work, his emphasis on the creative unknown vibrates with it. Unconscious to unconscious, psyche to psyche, mind to mind – so much permeates and enriches. This book opens many doors and passageways and gives us much to think about, experience and digest."

– **Michael Eigen**, *PhD,*
National Psychological Association for Psychoanalysis and
New York University Postdoctoral Program in
Psychotherapy and Psychoanalysis

Lacan and Chan Buddhist Thought

Reflections on Buddhism in Lacan's Seminar X and Beyond

Raul Moncayo and Yang Yu

Routledge
Taylor & Francis Group

LONDON AND NEW YORK

Cover image: © Getty Images

First published 2023
by Routledge
4 Park Square, Milton Park, Abingdon, Oxon OX14 4RN

and by Routledge
605 Third Avenue, New York, NY 10158

Routledge is an imprint of the Taylor & Francis Group, an informa business

© 2023 Raul Moncayo and Yang Yu

British Library Cataloguing-in-Publication Data
A catalogue record for this book is available from the British Library

ISBN: 978-1-032-05696-8 (hbk)
ISBN: 978-1-032-05697-5 (pbk)
ISBN: 978-1-003-19876-5 (ebk)

DOI: 10.4324/9781003198765

Typeset in Times New Roman
by Apex CoVantage, LLC

Contents

Preface

This book was inspired by Lacan's comments on Chan Buddhism in his Seminar X on Anxiety, as well as by our common interest in Chinese and Korean culture and language. *Lacan and Chan Buddhist Thought* continues and develops what Roudinesco (1997) called Lacan's fascination with the Far East.

We hope that psychoanalysts interested in Buddhism, as well as Chinese and Korean psychoanalytic practitioners and researchers, will feel especially at home when reading Lacan from a Chan perspective. We believe that this orientation in studying Lacan represents a form of psychoanalysis with unique East Asian characteristics. Lacanians or analysts not familiar with Lacan's later work may also find it helpful to understand the late Lacan with the help of Chan Buddhism. In particular Chan Buddhism broaches Lacan's classification of the Real, first as representing the destruction and devastation of the symbolic world, and later, as the link that fixes the three registers into a new knot of four.

Moncayo has reviewed the history of the relationship between psychoanalysis and Buddhism in a prior more general book on Zen and psychoanalysis. For a sample of the field of psychoanalysis and Buddhism, we refer readers to Safran's *Psychoanalysis and Buddhism* (2003), and, appearing nine years after, Moncayo's *The Signifier Pointing at the Moon* (2012). The current book is a sequel to this latter book and examines the internal and historical relations between psychoanalysis, a product of Western modernity, and Chan Buddhism as a fundamental philosophy and religious tradition central to Chinese language, culture, and thought.

We link free association in psychoanalysis to what Heidegger (1966), following Zen, called a quiet meditative form of thinking. But can Western thought really raise the question of non-thinking as a form of thought without the experience of meditation and from a philosophical point of view? This is a challenge Lacan poses to Western philosophy and science in a uniquely Chan moment in which he argues that thought is a form of jouissance. Taking up this challenge, we consider this book "a form of thinking at the end of Greek philosophy with an Eastern and topological twist of the knot" (Moncayo, 2021, p. 276).

Yang Yu is the sole author of Chapter 9, "The Paradoxical Chan Koans, Self-Reference, and Letter Jouissance." It reflects her long-term interest in the logical, mathematical, and philosophical roots of psychoanalysis. Professor Yu brings to the work not only her interest in the work of Hofstadter, in its relations to the use of paradox in Chan Buddhism and Lacanian theory, but also her studies on the emergence of the "I" as a form of psychical genesis.

Raul Moncayo has spent 40 years studying and practicing psychoanalysis and Chan Buddhism, experiencing their similarities and differences, and receiving transmission from both traditions. He began his studies of psychoanalysis in Buenos Aires and later was a founder of the Lacanian School of Psychoanalysis in San Francisco. He has studied psychoanalysis with people in the direct lineages of both Freud and Lacan and is a Chan descendant of Shunryo Susuki Roshi through his late teacher Sojun Roshi (Mel Weitsman) of Berkeley, California. In 2019, he founded the Blue Mountain Zen Center of El Cerrito in California.

We note this lineage because, beyond institutions and organizations, Chan and psychoanalysis rely on a personal, mind-to-mind transmission between analyst and analysand, teacher and student. In addition, Raul Moncayo, Yang Yu, and Hong Zhou together have founded the Beijing Center for Freudian and Lacanian Psychoanalysis and Research to transmit a Lacanian psychoanalysis with an ongoing, active engagement with Chinese culture.

Introduction

The occasion for Lacan's (1962–1963) reflections on Zen or Chan Buddhism in Seminar X is his encounter with Buddhist statues during his visit to the women's monastery of Todai-Ji at Nara in Japan. This was not the first time a psychoanalyst would discuss a work of art since Freud (1914) had famously discussed the Moses of Michelangelo. Lacan observed that

> It might strike you as surprising that I should qualify in this way statues that have a religious function, statues that were not in principle made with an eye to representing works of art. This, however, is incontestably what they are in their intention and their origin.
>
> (1962–1963, p. 222)

As if directly engaging this distinction between a work of art and "a religious function," Lacan notes that these Buddhist statues in Nara also have a "function."

> It is not therefore irrelevant for us to take this inroad to get something from them that leads us, I won't say to their message, but to what they can represent of a certain relationship between the human subject and desire. It can be found in the women's monastery, the *Chugu-ji* nunnery in Nara which was the seat of imperial power for several centuries, until the tenth century (p. 222). "It is one of these statues, one of the most beautiful, the one which is found in the women's monastery of *Todai-Ji*. I will tell you in a moment what function is involved.
>
> (Lacan, trans. by Gallagher, 8.5.63 XVII 154)[1]

In Section XVI, it is in the context of Lacan's reflections on Chan that we find that the statues raise the questions of desire and represent the Buddhist truth that desire is an illusion and the root cause of suffering. In the early form of the Buddhist teaching, or the first turning of the Dharma Wheel, this principle is known as the second noble truth. The first truth is that life is suffering since anxiety is not only the sign of an illness, but also an existential condition. Everyone suffers from anxiety, and, this way, anxiety approximates what early Buddhism refers to as the first noble truth that life is suffering. Anxiety represents both ordinary and pathological forms of suffering.

In Lacanian terms, the Buddhist concept of desire demonstrates how the *objet a* is the root object or cause of anxiety, a form of causality in the form of a gap or a lack, as Lacan would say in Seminar XI. Something anxiety-producing appears in the place/space of absence where nothing should be. Lacan's unique interpretation of the Buddhist concept of desire, in relationship to the object of anxiety, is crucial to the development of his own theory of desire.

When Lacan asks, "What does it mean, that desire is an illusion?" and answers that "The illusion here cannot but be referred to the register of truth" (Lacan, 2014, p. 222), he stresses that desire itself is not simply an illusion. The illusions of desire refer not to desire itself but to how metonymic objects of desire continually cover over the lack or void left by the absence of the logical *objet a* cause of desire. Because the *objet a* as cause of desire is structurally missing, Lacan speaks of the truth of desire as the fact that the objects of desire have a fictional structure (Illusory). This book follows Lacan's focus, then, on the illusions created by the objects of desire rather than simply qualifying desire itself as an illusion.

From this perspective, the objects of desire are illusions but not desire itself. Pure desire is an enigmatic affect that reveals the emptiness of the lack (of the object cause of desire) as an index of jouissance. The index refers to a basic form of the signifier. The index, however, appears to be more of a sign, or even an icon/image, than a signifier, while it does not exist outside the signifying system. It appears that the index, as the letter, is as close as the signifier gets to the jouissance and the Real outside the signifier. The difference between the sign and the letter is that the sign appears to be related to the object and icon. The letter instead falls entirely inside the signifying net that is cast over the entire object world.

In the classical Chan example of the finger and the moon, the index finger is used to represent the concepts and signifiers that we use to describe iconic objects such as the moon. The *Línjì* school uses this example to show how words about enlightenment are not the real moon of enlightenment. But for the Chan School, the Real moon of enlightenment is not the image of an object. The objective moon in the sky is not the hazy Real moon of enlightenment. Instead, the Real refers to the objective moon as a form of transsubjective jouissance beyond language. Illumination, free from objectivity and causation, becomes a wonder.

The index, then, does not refer to "the proximity/contiguity or similarity with the object. Proximity in this sense does not point to the physical presence of the object but rather to the subjective proximity of the object in the light of its absence" (Moncayo, 2018, p. 51). The analyst may be in physical proximity to the analysand, but the object that the analyst represents for the analysand may lie far away, yet near the transferential heart of the analysand's experience. The imaginary unconscious objects of the analysand are all marked by absence and loss. Because the object cause of desire is absent, the analysand tries to close the gap left by the absence of the object with the figure of the analyst. In the transference, how the analyst appears as the *objet a* is an illusion spun and fanned by language itself.

A fantasy object, for example, represents revised (secondary revision, according to Freud's interpretation of dreams) ways of representing the truths of desire that manifest according to the logical structure of the signifier. Metaphor and metonymy involved in the production of dreams and fantasies (illusions) represent the truths of desire albeit in hidden and distorted ways.

These truths of desire offer a view on Lacan's development of the concept of jouissance. For example, desire stops the inconvenience of the "first jouissance of the Other," otherwise known as the imaginary fusion with the mother, so that desire can be reached in the inverted ladder of the Law of symbolic castration. Under this law, desire and phallic jouissance function within the legitimacy of a Symbolic order, such that the Law of symbolic castration itself is also an index of jouissance.

Jouissance can represent satisfaction or suffering, something pleasant or unpleasant. The signifier and desire operating according to the pleasure principle want to lower the tensions associated with jouissance, particularly when jouissance is understood according to Lacan's early conception as inconvenient and destructive. The signifier and the Symbolic stop this inconvenient jouissance so that a desire can be reached that is compatible with the Law, while this desire is linked to the experience of phallic jouissance, or what is enjoyable and painful about phallic jouissance and sexuality.

However, Lacan reveals how phallic jouissance also fails to represent a form of satisfaction since it is always a question of who is or is not, does or does not have the phallus. The symbolic phallus is an absence, and symbolic castration functions as a portal for the satisfaction associated with the Third jouissance. The Third jouissance has three forms that function outside the Symbolic (phallic) order. These three are feminine jouissance, the jouissance of the mystic, and the jouissance of meaning.

"The Lotus of the True Law," the title of a central Mahayana sutra mentioned by Lacan, exemplifies the operations of jouissance. Within the Symbolic order and the Borromean knot, desire is caused by imaginary objects of desire (*objet a*). But a pure desire under the Law, while stopping the First jouissance, also allows for phallic jouissance (the Second jouissance) and represents an opening to the Real of the Third jouissance. Jouissance, like Truth as a form of jouissance, can be convenient or inconvenient, pleasant, or unpleasant. The First is initially pleasant, but then becomes inconvenient or addictive. The Second phallic jouissance can be pleasant or unpleasant, and the Third is mostly pleasant, if not at least equanimous and magnanimous.

Moving away from a common understanding of early Buddhism, psychoanalysis analyses rather than represses the imaginary of wishing and desire, and the relations between desire and the different forms of jouissance. Specifically, Lacan suggests an understanding of desire through the later Mahayana Buddhist tradition. Following these suggestions, this book explores how the bliss of Nirvana or of emptiness is not the product of the extinction of desire, but the very nature of desire as a form of a third Other jouissance. Desire and Nirvana, desire and the

Third jouissance, are neither one nor two. Desire and Nirvana do not extinguish each other, nor are they the same thing. Nirvana, as sublimation, stops the replication of the *objet a* (the infinite search for metonymic objects of desire) but does not extinguish desire, while the objects of desire cannot lead desire to Nirvana.

The early Theravada teaching said that Nirvana is the extinction or the opposite of desire, while Nagarjuna says they are both equally empty. However, when desire and Nirvana are confused as One, or the garden of Eden is interpreted as a form of pleasure, then this One is an imaginary One rather than what Lacan calls the real One's own non-being. The One of the Imaginary is not the One of the Real: "There is nothing more dangerous than confusion over what is involved in the One. The One is not Eros as fusion, making one from two" (Lacan [1972–1973], p. 91). The Imaginary One represents the fusion with the mother based on the imaginary object, while the One of the Real requires zero and non-being to manifest. Therefore, we think that it is more accurate to say that desire and Nirvana are neither one nor two.

Lacan, and his Parisian intellectual milieu in general, had a keen interest in Buddhism and Asian culture (the examples of Claude Lévi-Strauss and Roland Barthes immediately come to mind). In fact, in Seminar XXIII on the Sinthome, Lacan (1975–1976) calls himself *Jaclaque* Han.

This Chinese meaning and use of "Han" (韩) should be distinguished from the Korean meanings, pictograms, and use of the word "Han" (汉). As an ancient native Korean word, "Han" predates the adoption of the Chinese system of writing into the Korean "hanja" system of writing and means "great" and "Korean." As well, Korean "Han" is a homophone for various geographical and historical references, with different associated hanja characters, including the well-known reference to "Han" as a culturally distinct emotional state of unresolvable grief (恨). Grief becomes unsolvable when the lack (*laquehan*) is not identified and grieved.

Historically, Europeans and Chinese certainly associated "foreigner" with negative judgments at different times. The term Oriental, for example, is regarded by many in the West to represent the Othering of Asian cultures as exotic and irrational. In a similar way, in ancient China, such terms as *Manyi* (蛮夷) and *Yidi* (夷狄) were also used to refer to other small tribes or small minority groups outside the central plain region of China to imply their barbaric Otherness. The further away other tribes were from the center of China (the Middle Kingdom or 中), the more barbaric the tribes were thought to be. Barbarism was defined as the power of brute force and instinct as distinct from the power of a legitimate principle guiding the course of civilization.

In contrast to a history of mutual European and Asian Othering of each other, we would like to focus on a more ordinary Other, embedded in the Chinese notion of "Han and foreigner," simply meaning the Other *of*, instead of *in*, society, culture, and language. Other in this case does not have to have a negative imaginary connotation (φ and $-\varphi$), as in "We are civilized, and you are barbarians," or "Ours is better than yours." In other words, we take up "Han" and its connotation of a psychoanalytic Other as the unconscious. For Lacanians, the Han as Other, means both the Unconscious and language. "*Laquehan*" as a name is a play on the linguistic and cultural function of Han in Chinese by signaling both the group identity of a people and identity's lack as Other.

At stake in focusing on Lacan's engagement with Buddhism is the elaboration of the ethical implications of psychoanalysis for theorizing beyond cultural identities. For psychoanalysis, the cultural Other is always seen through the symbolic lens of the Unconscious and the subject of the Unconscious. The Other is an aspect of the subject, not outside the subject. This prevents the "Othering" of the Other, as if the Other has nothing to do with the subject (the opposing clan, nation, race, sex, etc., for example). Lacan was the founder of a group designation that represents something different than a cultural "Us and Them" othering. "Us and Them" thinking is attempting to close the gap in the ego through an imaginary group identification that could represent, for example, the danger of nationalism, and the logic of domination, as seen in the example of Nazi Germany. Self-designation in *Jacques "Lack-Han,"* or Nomination against identification, is revelatory of the subject of the lack. The ethical aspect of unconscious lack is that it prevents the lack from being "Othered" or attributed to a cultural Other.

Note

1 This text will use the English text edited by Miller, except when Gallagher's translation proves to be a better match with Chan Buddhist understanding, or when Miller has deleted portions of Lacan's transcribed oral teaching.

Chapter 1

Lacan and Vasubhandu
(世亲菩萨)

Indeed, Lacan's general interest in Buddhism, which may have taken him to Japan in the first place, went beyond his interest in Buddhist art.

> I was fated to travel by the right paths and I analyzed with my good mentor Demieville in those years when psychoanalysis left me more spare time, the book called *The Lotus and the True Law*, which was written into Chinese by Kumarajiva to translate a Sanskrit text. This text is more or less the historical turning point at which occurred the peculiar metamorphosis I'm going to ask you to keep in mind, namely, when Avalokitesvara, *he who hears the world's laments*, transforms – from the time of Kumarajiva, who seems to have been somewhat responsible for it – into a female divinity. She is called—I think you are at least slightly on the same wavelength—*Guanyin* (观音) or *Guan-shiyin*（观世音)—. This name is linked to the same meaning as the name Avalokitesvara carries, – *she who is considerate, who goes, who accords.* Here, is *Guan*.
>
> (1962–1963, p. 225)

Lacan goes on to make the additional point that humans are in little accord or harmony with a bodhisattva's compassion, even though the bodhisattva agrees with humans. Human disagreement with a bodhisattva equals their disagreement with each other. And, if humans would agree with bodhisattvas, then they might also agree with each other.

Despite a human rejection of compassion because of a definitional misunderstanding, a bodhisattva remains in agreement with others regardless of an apparent unfairness or injustice. In this regard, a bodhisattva differs from being a figure of the Law. A bodhisattva represents the Buddha's compassion where, although a subject may be in the wrong, a bodhisattva remains on his or her side because a spark of Buddha-nature can always be found or lit in any being.

Lacan is particularly interested in the bodhisattva Mahayana ideal represented by Avalokiteśvara and his ability to transform into a feminine form, perhaps to draw an analogy between the analyst and Avalokiteśvara who hears the cries of the world. Lacan argued that the position of the analyst is necessary to undo the Oedipal knot

DOI: 10.4324/9781003198765-1

of three and retie it into a knot of four. This undoing becomes possible through the listening of the analyst who hears how the Symbolic or ego holds the knot of three together and fails to reconcile its own struggle with the Id and the Imaginary, as well as the struggle between the Id and the super-ego, or between the Imaginary and the Real. While the Id represents libidinal ties between people, the first Real breaks them into traumatically unsymbolizable remainders. However, the retying of this undone knot of three into a knot of four also becomes possible through Lacan's reconceptualization of the relationship between the Real, the Ego, and the NoF. This new Real, which makes links, redoubles into a fourth cord or a new NoF. This new NoF, which holds the knot of four together, is what Lacan refers to as the sinthome, or a new ego in the Real.

Both the analyst and the bodhisattva know that many things in the life of the subject can serve the function of the new NoF, as opposed to an external traditional figure of the Law. Indeed, even suffering resulting from the mistakes of the subject can provide the fuel and manure for the subject's evolution and transformation via the symptom.

Just as the position of the analyst is a site or figure of the sinthome, Lacan suggests that the bodhisattva, too, is like the sinthome (condensation of symptom and *saint homme*) since the bodhisattva is a human being who has renounced his or her personal enlightenment to help others first. The diamond sutra defines the beneficent activity of a bodhisattva as "no one" being helped and no "one" helping. The bodhisattva's compassion is not altruistic. Freud (1915) observed in his paper "On Drives and their Vicissitudes" that even non-self-centered altruism can easily represent and revert to egoism. This corresponds to why historically the colonizer experiences colonization in terms of altruism, while the colonized experience it in terms of the egoism and self-interest of the colonizer.

An example of a topological accord between bodhisattvas and human beings can be taken from the legendary relations between the leaders of the three religions in China for which Han or Chan Buddhism represents an amalgamation. Chan is a combination of Mahayana Buddhism, Taoism, and Confucianism. Lao Tzi, Kong Tzi (Confucius), and Bodhidharma or Buddha are legendarily depicted as three friends having a deep conversation in a natural landscape and enjoying each other's company. The historical Buddha was a contemporary of Lao Tzi and Kong Tzi, and Bodhidharma brought Chan to China around 400 CE.

In these traditions, the very definition of the human (Ren) is defined from the perspective of the heart of compassion and friendship. This is in stark contrast to the violence associated with Western religions and their historical conflicts with one another. Western religions from this perspective appear to be "human all too human" in the bad sense of being only human and without the capacity to create accord between their traditions and human beings outside and belonging to other traditions. Having said this, and despite the peaceful coexistence of the leaders of the three Chinese traditions, there have of course been conflicts between followers, as well as alliances with government to achieve political hegemony within the culture.

In the development of his theory of subjectivity centered around the Real of jouissance, Lacan seems to have borrowed from Mahayana Buddhist Yogachara teaching to offer this second definition of the Real operating within a Borromean knot of four. In this sense, Lacan's reference to the Lotus Sutra (《莲华经》), functions as a metonymy to signify more fundamental interests in Buddhism. In *The Signifier Pointing at the Moon*, Moncayo (2012) noted the similarity between Lacan's three registers and the threefold aspect of self-nature taught by Indian Mahayana Buddhist ancestor Vasubhandu (third century CE).

Vasubhandu (Anacker, 1984b) referred to the threefold aspect of self-nature as the Imagined, the Other-dependent, and the Real. The Imagined is another word for the Imaginary, and the "Other-dependent" is not too far from Lacan's symbolic Other. Significantly, the Real in Vasubhandu would be closer to the second Real in Lacan. The second Real remains a form of experience and jouissance linked to the NoF in the knot of four and to convenient and civilizing forms of the death drive and jouissance.

Some might dismiss this apparent coincidence of ideas between Vasubhandu and Lacan in different cultural contexts as a pattern or structure, or even an archetype in the Jungian sense. We think it more likely that Lacan hid the influence of Vasubhandu's Yogachara teaching on his work to erase any association with something other than secular or scientific philosophic traditions. With these comments, we do not intend to criticize Lacan for not acknowledging his indebtedness to Vasubhandu because if what is discussed next is true, then Lacan put Vasubhandu's knowing to good use within the context of contemporary scientific and psychoanalytic culture. What is clear is that Lacan engaged and turned a teaching linked to a meditational practice to a topological concept consistent with contemporary mathematics and the principles of psychoanalysis.

Lacan's first definition of the Real remains important, however, because it is the properly Freudian psychoanalytic concept that obviously was not part of Vasubhandu's trefoil knot. This first Real is hazardous, ominous, uncanny, terrible, and unsymbolizable in a traumatic way and has an intrinsic connection to destructive aspects of the drive. By being unsymbolizable, the Real constituted a threat to the coherence of the Symbolic order. The first Real was also a sign of things not working well or going wrong or awry. This Real was disruptive and destructive of links within language and between people. If the Real broke links rather than made them, then the Symbolic was responsible for reining-in this form of the Real. However, Lacan finds that the Symbolic does not do this well because subjects are involved in a struggle also with the Imaginary.

In his earlier thought, Lacan used the term "real" interchangeably with a notion of the real in Freud's reality principle. To disambiguate these two terms in Lacan's thinking, we capitalize the Real to differentiate it from social and environmental reality. This differentiation is necessary to follow a certain line of thought between Lacan's early discussion of the real, and his later teachings. In Seminar XXII, RSI, we eventually find Lacan's argument that the Borromean knot is what establishes the difference between reality and the Real. The knot is mathematically

Real rather than a social or environmental reality. This second articulation of the Real is the knot itself rather than simply one of its three dimensions, which we would now refer to as the first Real. When Lacan says that "The Real only has 'ex-sistence' . . . by encountering the arrest of the Symbolic and the Imaginary" (Lacan, 1955–1956, B. III, p. 7), this is his second conceptual articulation of the Real, which mediates social reality and holds the knot together. This is the Real of jouissance and topology rather than the Symbolic. To change that which is experienced as the impossible aspect of social reality, or the first Real, into possibility, the structure of the knot must be changed first via the second Real.

This is how we arrive at the second Real as a Real that now makes accord rather than breaking links. Referring to this operation, Lacan says that "The Real is a third" (Lacan [1975–1976], Session of 9.12.75, II XIV). What does he mean by this?

If Lacan's earlier reference to the Third was the Symbolic that tied and symbolized the imaginary relation to the Real, the second Real as a Third reties the Imaginary to the Symbolic. In the first knot of three, the Real is tied by the Symbolic to the Imaginary. Here, the Real is seen through the lens of the Imaginary, and the Third is that which ties the two together. Thus, the Symbolic Third. However, in the second knot of three, the Third is the Real because it ties the Imaginary to the Symbolic and the Symbolic receives its structure from the Real. Thus, the "Real is third," and from this structure comes the NoF that will be a fourth ring that reties the knot of three into four.

The second Real makes links rather than breaks them and relieves the Symbolic from being responsible for maintaining the structure of the Borromean knot. Lacan goes as far as saying that the small points or strings of the Real have a stronger consistency than the Imaginary and that it was time for the Real to reappropriate the consistency of the knot from the Imaginary. Although the Symbolic and the Law make links within language, they are also involved in a bitter struggle reining in the Imaginary into the structure of the knot. In the case of psychosis, the Imaginary prevails and remains loose outside the knot.

The Real is equidistant to both and for this reason is in a better position to cajole the Symbolic and the Imaginary into cooperation. Moreover, to perform this new function, the Real must be duplicated in such a way that the second Real that would tie the Borromean knot of four is no longer the Real of the knot of three. The disruptive role of the Real in the knot of three has been changed to the reparative and constructive function of the second Real as a new organ in the knot of four.

The second Real is also known as the Name of the Father that comes out of the Real of *savior* and jouissance (and no longer from the Symbolic or knowledge alone). The new Name has more to do with Nomination than metaphor, substitution, or symbolization. Nomination points to the Real of the body and jouissance, making a symbolic hole in the process, since the signified now is in the Real rather than the Symbolic (S_0 rather than S_2).

The Symbolic makes a hole in the Real, as Lacan often said, in the sense that the signifier in the body functioning as signified appears as an absence of an S_2

that could define and close the meaning of the S_1 signifier linked to the Name. Is this hole Symbolic or Real?

Ordinarily, the Symbolic makes a hole in the Real in a specific way. The Real is constituted in a thing as "no-thing" outside the signifier but is replaced with the signifier, thus, splitting the thing-in-itself in the process. From now on, the thing-in-itself will lie outside the signifier, and the signifying network is laid upon the entire object world. According to Lacan, the Real of jouissance outside the signifier is a plenum without anything missing, and the hole refers to how the Real appears in the Symbolic as a lack of a signifier. The signifier for the thing-in-itself is missing within the Symbolic. The absence of a signifier for the Real "no-thing" allows for the Real instead to be lodged in the body in lieu of where the mental signifier would have been in the mind. Instead of meaning being defined by an S_1–S_2 relation between signifiers, meaning here is a function of the Third jouissance when the signified is in the Real of bodily jouissance. The new NoF that is ejected out of the Real, is the father of the Name, as well as the sinthome, while its signified resides in the body of the subject.

The sinthome is the place of the subject (of jouissance) and the symptom within the knot, while the sinthome shows how the subject can be confused for the Real that makes the knot. It is the Real that makes the knot, not the subject, although as sinthome, and as a second form of the Real, the subject can aspire not to make the knot, or in other words, to "know-how" (*savior faire*) to work within a topological process involving the circulation of signifiers according to various forms of jouissance.

For the second Real, what is unthinkable about the Real is no longer traumatic and serves the function of non-thinking and non-knowing that helps the subject live within uncertainty. What used to be impermanence or decay, or things falling apart, are now obstacles that facilitate the evolution of the subject. Thus, the Real can be thought of as having two faces, but only insofar as they are not reduced to simplistic definitions of good and evil. The Real, Lacan says in Seminar XXIII, is without Law and is beyond good and evil although it appears in both.

Hinting how he may have come across Vasubhandu's threefold knot in Seminar X, Lacan mentions his Buddhist "master" by name: Demiéville. Demiéville's (1954) familiarity with the Yogachara teaching of Vasubhandu can be seen in his translation of Yogachara writings. As well, the fact that Vasubhandu's Yogachara teaching from 300 CE corresponds with the same period of Plotinus (204–270 CE), the Egyptian neo-Platonic philosopher who influenced Lacan's Seminar XIX on the One's own non-being, further suggests the importance of Chinese and Buddhist philosophy on Lacan's development of the Real.

Chapter 2

The Second Turning of the Dharma Wheel

Nagarjuna's Teachings on Nirvana

To further trace the influence of Buddhist philosophy on Lacan's thought, from Freud's own references to Lacan's developments, we now turn our focus to how Lacan gives new significations to the second noble truth that desire is the cause of suffering, and the third noble truth that Nirvana is the extinction of desire.

In addition to inheriting Freud's eye for religious statues, Lacan also inherited Freud's engagement with the Buddhist concept of Nirvana. In *Beyond the Pleasure Principle*, Freud (1920) references the earlier Theravada Buddhist idea of Nirvana to conceptualize the bringing down of excitations to level zero. The idea of Nirvana, defined as the extinction of desire, would later be redefined by Nagarjuna (100 CE) as emptiness. Nagarjuna's teachings are considered by scholars of Buddhism as the second turning of the Dharma Wheel. In this new teaching, earlier Theravada teachings of the four noble truths, including the idea of Nirvana, are reinterpreted.

Nagarjuna taught that Samsara is Nirvana and Nirvana, Samsara. Samsara is the world or wheel of desires and suffering, or in other words, the repetition compulsion, caused by unforeseen consequences associated with karma and the Law, or the unintended consequences of our actions. Nirvana is the gate of bliss and realization, or of something new and surprising that breaks the chains of compulsive repetition (*Tyche*). There is an intrinsic relation between joy and pain, between the ordeals linked to bliss and realization, and the pleasures linked to suffering. For Nagarjuna, this relation is given in the fact that both Nirvana and Samsara are empty or share the void as nature's default state.

The satisfaction of desire is never about the object of desire that we seem to immediately want. We usually put forth contradictory demands to the other: "I ask that you give me what I want" but also "I ask that you do not give me what I want because if you do, my desire and enjoyment will not only be fulfilled but also extinguished." The imbrication of the drives also appears within this dynamic of desire. The object of the drive both satisfies the drive, and if the object of the drive is also the *objet a*, which is meant to be lost, then the satisfaction of the demand for the *objet a* leaves desire asking for more (replicating the *a*), or extinguishing desire for the object (so to speak) because desire was not for or about the object. In this case, the pursuit of the object is abandoned.

DOI: 10.4324/9781003198765-2

Once the subject gets what he or she wants, the object loses its appeal and may turn into aversion or even hate. Getting what we want is not always satisfying. Contemporary Zen teacher Suzuki (1970, untranscribed talk) Roshi used to say: "Be careful with what you want because you may get it and may not like it." Contrary to the Hinayana or Theravada view, desire is extinguished not only by its denial but also by its satisfaction, because desire was not about the object. Conversely, desire is perpetuated when it is denied. Because we want what we can't have or don't have, if we are told we cannot have it, it only intensifies the desire. The illusions of desire lead us to want what we can't have or don't have, and to not want what we have. This illusion in turn is built on another illusion that the Other has something that we don't, or that the subject has something that the other does not. In either case, the Other does not exist, as Lacan says.

Finally, it is important to "re-cognize" that the void, vacuum, sunyata, or emptiness cannot be defined as, or turned into a metaphysics. "Nagarjuna was careful to warn that emptiness is a heuristic, not a cognitive, notion" (Loy, 1992, p. 234). Sunyata, like "*différance*," is permanently under erasure (Derrida, 1978). Lacan would say Nirvana does not cease from not being written. Emptiness is "deployed for tactical reasons but denied any semantic or conceptual stability" (Loy, 1992) against a background of related concepts within language. Emptiness is a bridge concept between the concept and the non-concept, between the Symbolic and the Real, between the signifier and jouissance, between identity and non-identity, between language and the experience of jouissance outside concepts and the signifier.

Joy and pain, suffering and realization, for example, are concepts and non-conceptual experiences that define the antithetical Lacanian concept of jouissance. Jouissance is a word that contains opposite meanings. Differences among words and concepts help us understand the contingent nature of phenomenal events (i.e., joy and pain), while the concept of emptiness helps us realize how joy and pain are "transformations" of a jouissance outside language that structures linguistic relations. Logic is established only when it disappears and becomes emptiness. Lacanian "Truth," rather than what is true about a proposition, depends on the emptiness or jouissance of the author as the foundation of the statement.

Nagarjuna elucidates emptiness by means of a language that is not the ego's own or does not belong to the ego of the author. It is the nonexistence of the imaginary ego that provides a foundation for the signifier as a subject without substance. As Lacan said, the subject fades before the signifier. A signifier or subject flies, moves, or shifts within the chain of signifiers, in the same way that a bird flies without self-consciousness of the air or themselves. As Lacan also stated, "I think where I am not" or "I think where the ego is not the one doing the thinking." In this case, "I (in the sense of me or my ego) am not the I that is doing the thinking," or "Where 'I' thinks, me or my ego is not." The I or *Je* applies to both the signifier as a shifter, and to the subject of jouissance.

There are two different truths within Lacanian theory that Lacan borrowed from Heidegger and that coincidentally also were part of Nagarjuna's teaching in the first century CE. The first Truth is in the Real of jouissance, while the second truth operates at the level of the signifier, a proposition, or a representation. Objective truth in formal logic is defined as the correspondence between a proposition and its object. This is the thing-in-itself or the Absolute in science. For us, as well as Nagarjuna, this is the second truth or principle. The first truth or principle, the "no-thing," or thing-in-itself, is the correspondence not between number or language statement and object, but the correspondence between number, statement, knowing, and "*Jouis-Sense*."

In general, we would say that Truth, as something Real within the Symbolic, involves "*J'ouis-Sense*" or one of the forms of the Third jouissance that has an intrinsic link to language, not as communication or information, but as a conveyer of signification. The other two forms of the Third Other jouissance are feminine jouissance and the jouissance of the mystic. *J'ouis-Sense*, or what Lacan called "*L'troisieme*," in his paper of the same name, has also been called the jouissance of meaning.

This presents the problem of whether we are to understand this form of jouissance as meaning in the Imaginary or Real. In Seminar XXI, "The 'Unduped' wander/are Mistaken" (as translated by Gallagher from the French, "*Les Non-Duped Errant*"), Lacan indirectly responds to this problem. In this seminar, he uses the riddle as the paradigm for the fullness of meaning. The riddle is the most condensed place for signifiers, which exist only as a tail or a track of sounds. Fullness, as emptiness and senselessness, rather than completeness or too much double meaning, is something Real rather than Imaginary. The One's own non-being is predicated by phonematic identity and veiled meaning indicated by the title of Seminar XXI. The "'unduped' make mistakes" ("*Les Non-Duped Errant*"), in French, sounds like the Name of the Father (*Les noms du-père*). What the homophony of sound knows about the link between the two terms is a riddle or an enigma. Rather than a conventional link, sound as an element inside language and yet outside functions as what turns being duped into a signified of the signifier of the NoF. Sound turns the signifier into something Real in the Lacanian sense of *J'ouis-Sense*.

One must allow oneself at times to be duped by the NoF and the symbolic function in order not to make more serious mistakes in life. Symbolic castration cannot be avoided, while the father of the family does not have to be perfect to exercise his function. A subject must tolerate symbolic castration even though it may be unpleasant or appear in fantasy as imaginary forms of castration. Acceptance here includes tolerating a few inconsistencies and lack in the Other, because if these are not accepted and instead are used to refuse symbolic castration and the function of the father, then subjects will make more serious mistakes in life that destructively play out in the symbolic and social order.

Chapter 3

Rereading Freud's Nirvana

How to think, then, of Freud's reference to Nirvana, given Nagarjuna's more complex teaching on Nirvana as Samsara and Samsara as Nirvana? There are glimpses of Nirvana within Samsara or the truths of desire, and Nirvana cannot be realized without the fertilizing raw material of Samsaric passions. Freud's discussion of Nirvana in *Beyond the Pleasure Principle*, like Nagarjuna's, can be read as a non-dual, paradoxical principle because the tendency toward drive satisfaction, or the elimination of tensions, associated with sexual intercourse (Psyche), stems from the same Mind linked to mental defenses against the drives. For example, sexual orgasm is both the temporary satisfaction of the drive, and of pleasurable tensions, as well as the culmination and extinction of unpleasant tensions. Mind and Psyche, defenses and the drives, like the Mobius strip, are neither one nor two, while being aspects of the same thing. Neither dualism nor monism apply to the drives in this case (the drive is "not-one/not-two").

Freud located the functioning of the Nirvana principle within the Mind, defined by a notion of Mind constituted by mental defenses, as well as a notion of the Psyche constituted by desire and the drives. Mental defenses lower tension and stress, if not to extinguish excitations, at least to reduce them to the lowest possible level and keep this tension/distension constant. He refers to this function as the constancy principle within reason, or reason with an openness for change, which we will discuss in greater detail in the next section.

For now, we note how meditation practice is often considered a form of defense against the cauldron of the drives and unpleasant levels of excitation and agitation. Drives, with their chemicals and signifiers, push subjects to what Buddhists regard as the poisons of greed, envy, hate, jealousy, and delusion. With meditation practice, these poisons are transformed into generosity, sympathetic joy, loving kindness, and enlightenment.

Approached in such a way, however, Chan or meditation and Nirvana, as symbolic defenses and processes, can also run counter to the analytic process of free association (for the analysand) and free-floating attention (for the analyst). For example, emptiness, as erasure or forgetting, and as a truth effect or operation, can run both alongside free association and counter to it. Meditation practice can become a form of "not-thinking," or thought repression and affect suppression that

DOI: 10.4324/9781003198765-3

stalls the symbolization of imaginary thinking in speech in the personal experience of analysis and works against the transformation of thinking and understanding into a smooth, free-thinking way of observation and experience.

Freud's reference to Nirvana opens the possibility of detailing a Chan, or Zen definition of free association in analysis. In free association, a soft and open mind, without stagnation or defensiveness, transforms a signifying "chain" into a more flexible and multidimensional Borromean knot. This could also serve as a definition for the kind of thinking in Buddhism called mindfulness. Mindfulness observes from within the experience of feeling and jouissance, and this adds an element of stability to cognition. If we are prepared to think in free association, then we do not have to make so much effort to think or write, for that matter. Thinking mindfully in this way is also a form of knowing that facilitates access to Unconscious knowing.

On the side of the analyst, a free-floating attention is also a form of mindfulness, but in the sense of a panoramic awareness that does not focus on any specific details of observation, yet knows exactly where anything significant may be within the narrative of the analysand. On this definition, mindfulness (one of the early teachings of the Buddha) cannot be restricted to a specific obsessional activity such as chewing a raisin a hundred times. This would be the equivalent of an analyst having a specific agenda that he or she wants the analysand to mull over. Instead, the analyst listens with a free-floating attention until the Unconscious makes its appearance in the analysand's speech and body movement.

Even as we acknowledge how emptiness and Nirvana can run both alongside and counter to free association, we propose adopting a specifically *Cáodòng*, or Chan approach to meditation to develop Freud's reference to Nirvana. Meditation in this tradition does not defend against the cauldron of the drives but instead encourages the practitioner to think freely without defensiveness or stagnation. The paradoxical Nirvana principle, extended to the labors of free association, on the one hand, engages the principle of the death drive that wants to bring down all excitation to level zero. In this sense, free association is a principle of mental discharge. Free association can lead to the undoing of repression, and to increased excitation, in preparation for a final release, only for tensions to begin accruing once again.

The reduction of tensions, on the other hand, represents a defense mechanism against the tensions and signifiers of the sexual drive and this may or may not be helpful in reducing excitation to level zero. The sexual drive wants to reduce tensions by temporarily increasing pleasant excitations, only to bring them down or extinguish them in sexual satisfaction. In the end, Freud suggests, and Lacan would later definitively show, that the sexual drive as a form of the pleasure principle works for the death drive.

Do the death drive and the pleasure principle both want the same thing, namely, increases and decreases of pleasant and unpleasant tensions? Are their operations of increasing and decreasing tensions paradoxical or contradictory? Lacan leads us toward an answer by showing us how the signifier works under the pleasure principle, as well as how the death drive operates toward something beyond the pleasant/unpleasant increases of tension. In fact, Lacan takes the irreducibility of the symbolic determination of the subject as one manifestation of the death drive. From this perspective, it becomes possible to grasp how the death drive works for the life drive insofar as the Symbolic order facilitates sexual reproduction within a system of symbolic exchanges. The displacements of the signifier are involved in the tendency to compulsively repeat past suffering and traumas, and at the same time, the signifier, Lacan says, is regulated by the pleasure principle so that desire can be reached through the inverted ladder of the Law.

One of the underappreciated moments in Freud's complex analysis of the relationship between the death and life drives is his reference to, in addition to the Nirvana and pleasure principles, the constancy principle. On the one hand, the task of living requires that tension and overstimulation, or suffering and trauma, be reduced and defended against by the pleasure principle. On the other hand, since the pleasure principle seeks to bring down all excitations to level zero – something that would coincide not only with pleasure but also death – the task of living in society also requires the postponement of both pleasure and death. What postpones both the pleasure principle and the death drive is the constancy principle, or the primary task of at least keeping the tensions as low as possible and keeping this level constant. Just like sexual tensions between two people may lead to the sexual act and to a final sexual discharge, the binding and tolerance of tensions throughout life, rather than their complete elimination, would prepare the tensions of life for their final elimination at the time of death.

Freud (1920) established an equivalence between the Nirvana principle, the pleasure principle, and the death drive and considers them the dominating impulses of mental life, and perhaps of nervous life in general. What they all have in common is an effort to keep constant or remove a certain level of internal tension due to stimuli (p. 50). Again, the pleasure principle here seems to work for the death drive (p. 57).

The key paradox in Freud's formulation we focus on here is whether the dominant impulse of the death drive is to seek libidinal pleasure and excitation or the elimination of tension, as defined by Freud; or to defend against painful or unpleasant tensions but not necessarily through sexual discharge or sexual satisfaction. Is the dominant tendency of the death drive to seek the elimination of tension through sexual pleasure, or to defend against painful or unpleasant tensions, but not necessarily through sexual discharge or sexual satisfaction?

In the latter case, the defense against pain is carried out by the constancy principle as a modification of the pleasure principle. For Freud, it is the constancy principle that reveals how the subject of the sexual drive tolerates a margin of pleasurable and unpleasant tensions and alternates between these and the lowering of tension. The constancy principle prepares the body for the final release at the time of both sex (temporary in this case) and, ultimately, death.

The constancy principle represents the workings of a productive or life-affirming rather than a nihilistic or destructive function of the death drive. The constancy principle, read with Freud's references to Nirvana, suggests that emptiness can be productive of a free association and openness to a playful freedom of the signifier unconstrained by defensiveness.

Indeed, when discussing the constancy principle, Freud concludes that either Nirvana or the death drive here works for the life drive or for life preservation. This seems to point to two different aspects of the death drive: a nihilistic and a life-affirming side. Perhaps this is no different from the distinction between an emptiness of presence (the Real as a plenum outside signification), and the emptiness of absence, as in the case of loss, depression, and character disorders.

Freud's recourse to the constancy principle to develop a notion of emptiness or zero that structures the death drive as both destructive and affirming allows us to now turn back to Lacan's development of three forms of jouissance, and three forms of the Third jouissance. The first jouissance of the Other refers to the dual imaginary union between mother and infant that can be both productive and unproductive. It becomes unproductive without the eventual intervention of the NoF or the Other, and its transformation into phallic jouissance. Phallic jouissance in turn needs to evolve into the Third jouissance but without abandoning symbolic phallic jouissance and while limiting its inconvenient surpluses and excesses.

Fantasy and the two Reals are also related, since fictions derive their strength from emptiness or inexistence, and the Imaginary often takes the place of the Real. The drives arise from the void, since, as we explore later, the void is nature's default state. Only with the Third, or the third form of jouissance, can jouissance remain productive albeit incomplete. Even though we, as Freud did, have been discussing the questions of the Nirvana principle in economic or energetic terms, it is important to remember that Nirvana or the Third jouissance also appears as a jouissance of meaning within language in forms of the riddle.

Indeed, Lacan's reference to Chan or Zen traditions more generally indicate an implicit indebtedness to a psychoanalytic concept of Nirvana that is more than simply the calming, lowering, or suppressing of tensions, or even the form of "quietism" that the *Línjì* or Rinzai school leveled as a critique against *Cáodòng* Chan or Soto Zen. Nirvana as death or the Real represents the Chan act of symbolically cutting a cat in two. Here we are referring to another famous Chan story in which master *Zhaozhou* (Nansen in Japanese), in response to two monks arguing over whom a cat belonged to, cut the cat in half. Nansen demanded that they utter a well-spoken word, and if the two monks failed to do so, he would cut the cat in two and give each of them one half. Since the monks could not utter well-spoken words, Nansen symbolically cut the cat in two to show them the consequences of their dualistic thinking and speech. This cut, which metaphorically kills the cat, also cuts through the monks' arguments based on their imaginary possession of the cat.

This story, interestingly, echoes the famous and older story of King Solomon in the Torah. In this story, at issue between the two mothers is not a cat, but a child. One of the mothers steps forward to tell the King to give the child to the other woman. She effectively relinquishes her claim to the child to stop the King from cutting the child in two. In contrast to the Chan story earlier, this mother was able to say a good word. In relinquishing her claim, she revealed her love for the child as a subject and gave up the child as her narcissistic possession. Because of this, King Solomon did not cut the child in two and was able to recognize the child's true mother.

The use of the Name (the King's authority) and the signifier (the good word) was enough to elicit the authenticity of the mother's desire in this story from the Torah. Interpreted through Lacanian theory, this is a parable of how certain symbolic acts, even while taking place at the level of the signifier, reveal a marriage between the second death and the signifier. The signifier, the good word spoken in the Torah, is demanded but not spoken in the Chan story and is metaphorically absent.

The signifier spoken by the teacher contains the power of life and death: "Speak the good word so you may live, otherwise you encounter the deadliness of the law." If the monks refuse to cut their imaginary discussions over the cat and fail to use speech to elevate the conversation to another level, the cat becomes a deadly object for them. This is a scenario in which the imaginary kills the word, while the death drive in the signifier gives rise to the living word. In this way, these two stories exemplify the paradoxical nature of the drives reflected in Freud's exploration of the Nirvana principle.

Chapter 4

The Pleasure, Constancy, and Nirvana Principles

In his *Project* (1895), Freud was following Fechner in seeking a physical and mental principle that would explain desire, dreams, and the serenity of the mind. He asked whether people are motivated by sexual desire or spiritual purposes. Spiritual purposes want to lower emotional tensions without abandoning pleasurable sexual tensions. Pain can be used for emotional growth and the development of character, and pleasure can be applied to the Law.

> Since we have a certain knowledge of a trend in psychical life towards avoiding, we are tempted to identify that trend with the primary trend towards inertia. In that case unpleasure would coincide with a rise in the level of quantity. . . . Pleasure would be the sensation of discharge.
>
> (Freud, 1895, p. 373)

Freud links inertia with the Nirvana principle, but he also links it with Fechner's concept of the constancy principle, briefly discussed earlier.

We note that Lacan does not take up Freud's discussion of the constancy principle. In fact, he eschewed this idea because he considered it a kind of "bourgeois" principle of the middle, or a false sense of security, detracting from an analysis of excesses. At the same time, the analytical task can only proceed according to a principle of equanimity that Freud referred to as neutrality in the face of being loved or hated in the transference, for example. The middle is not always in the middle, and the analyst's equanimity is not the analysand's ambivalence.

Success and failure provide another good example. We do not try to both fail and succeed at the same time, although it is true that we experience both in life. At the same time, we do not try to half-succeed and half-fail unless under a pathological influence. We accept rather than reject success, but at the same time do not cling to failure since it is never final. In this example, clinging to success or failure represents a mistaken understanding of the Nirvana principle. Instead, Nirvana in Buddhism is represented by equanimity and the constancy principle, but without thinking of it as an imaginary and bourgeois egoic principle rejected by Lacan. In

DOI: 10.4324/9781003198765-4

this section, we use an extended reading of the constancy principle in *Beyond the Pleasure Principle* to, on the one hand, further elucidate and evaluate the influence of Freud's Buddhist references in psychoanalysis, and on the other hand, to evaluate the influence of the mathematical and physical sciences in Lacan's later work on topology, and true and false vacuums and holes.

As often noted by his many readers, Freud's essay is enigmatic and replete with seeming contradictions and paradoxes. Our discussion, then, of several contradictions and paradoxes that emerge in Freud's discussion of the constancy principle focuses on analyzing these seeming contradictions and paradoxes through Nagarjuna's lens. Nagarjuna's lens also coincides with developments in contemporary Western philosophy, Lacanian psychoanalytic theory, and contemporary physics. In Chapter 9, for example, we offer a different approach or reading based on Gödel's mathematical theories. This is to say that our discussion of the idea of constancy inherited by psychoanalysis from physics, and other discussions on theoretical mathematics and the history of science, are necessary for further developing aspects of the later Lacan.

Before continuing to examine the Freudian principles under discussion, we dedicate a few pages now to contextualize Freud's references to developments in the science of physics and their more contemporary resonances in Lacan's own interests in science. In today's physics, the concept of zero-point energy (ZPE) would be the equivalent of what Freud, borrowing from the physics of his time, called the tendency of the mind to bring down excitations or energetic charges to level zero. ZPE refers to the lowest possible level of energy that a quantum system may have. A vacuum can be viewed not as empty space but as the combination of all zero-point fields. In quantum field theory, this combination of fields is called the vacuum state, its associated ZPE is called the vacuum energy, and the average energy value is called the vacuum expectation value. In cosmology, the vacuum energy is one possible explanation for Einstein's cosmological constant and the source of dark energy. In the vacuum state, energetic values above zero are fluctuating about their mean value of zero. For example, each value in its lowest point is not completely at rest but always is moving about its equilibrium position. Dark energy is a dark flow of the ZPE of the vacuum. The simplest explanation for dark energy is that it is an intrinsic, fundamental energy of space or the vacuum (www.askamathematician. com/2012/07/q-what-is-the-false-vacuum-and-are-we-living-in-it).

Zero-point energy fluctuates to the lowest possible state, which in turn, allows the formation of constant matter that sustains the material structure of the universe. What about the material structure of the Mind? It is interesting to consider the function played by the constancy principle in both Einstein and Freud. For Einstein, it was a question of finding an equilibrium for the universe since his formulas predicted that the universe would either expand to extinction or contract back perhaps to another fiery explosion. The cosmological constant provided a means for the universe to remain if not static, then at least stable. When the Hubble telescope showed that the universe was expanding, Einstein called the constancy principle his biggest blunder. However, since then, and as already stated, Einstein's constant is now considered similar or equivalent to vacuum dark energy that is the lowest possible level of energy a quantum system may have.

In Freud's writing, constancy refers to both the lowest possible level of energy that at the same time allows for the mind and its material constituents to exist and function. So, the constancy principle plays a similar function for Freud as it does for Einstein's cosmological constant. In fact, Freud may have borrowed this term from Einstein since they knew each other. It was Einstein who requested that a Freud chair be established at the Hebrew University in Jerusalem, which still exists today.

Lacan for his part may have rejected the constancy principle for similar reasons that Einstein thought it was his biggest blunder. The universe and the mind are not static. However, stability here is not the same as a static state. Stability and stillness and movement are always interacting. Stability occurs within movement and change, and movement takes place against a background of stillness and stability. Constancy and stability are provided by the vacuum dark energy at a level that allows for material and psychical reality to exist. This form of constancy, which includes some level of fluctuation or value above zero, is what allows matter to exist as such. The paradox here is that this value above zero is still zero and is the same paradox whereby the constancy principle still works for the Nirvana principle in Freud's theory.

It follows, then, that if we say that form or matter is emptiness, or exists in emptiness, this means that, to exist, matter requires a quantum field of dark energy with a value fluctuating above but also around zero. Matter exists in a field of ZPE or thereabouts. At the same time, if the value is reduced to a true zero, then the universe and the Mind vanish.

From the point of view of Lacanian theory, we can say that the observable universe of speech and discourse is an epiphenomenal "watermark" of a jouissance generated by vacuum states. The Real Unconscious as a true hole containing vacuum field waves of jouissance generates the letter as a watermark of jouissance at places of increased density or condensation in the field. These points of increased density also energize the function and purpose of the signifier, the word, and representation in general. As the neutron emerges from the vacuum state, so the letter emerges in the "littoral" between jouissance and the signifying elements or materials. The signifier emerges from a field of jouissance.

A field of jouissance represents an affective state/wave before a signifier can represent it. The same way that the vacuum has an incipient ability to create order and structure, jouissance outside the signifier can spray a glue that structures and creates links between signifiers. When a thought is created, the thought transitions out of a particular field of jouissance. Jouissance is what is unsayable about the field in which a thought emerges. A field is what both releases or gestates a thought and what absorbs it once the thought has been either spent or associated. Thought is a leap out of a zero state and back into the zero state.

In any physical system, we find an energy "ground zero state" that the system tries to approach. Water in a bathtub, for example, will be as low and still as possible. The mathematical term for this state of tub water is a "local energy minimum."

At the same time, what we may regard at any one moment in time or in the history of science as the "ground state," or a vacuum, will later be revealed not to be the true ground state.[1]

There is always the possibility that what we think is the ground state, the vacuum, may not be the true ground state and would instead be a "false vacuum." We think there is nothing there, a vacuum, but there is, in fact, something there. In this figure, this something is the water, and in contrast to the relatively lower dip in the surface, the higher dip filled with water would be a false vacuum. If the universe were to become a "true" vacuum, it would be the end of our universe as we know it because what is there, or the something (the water) in the nothing, allows for the universe to exist. In other words, if the something (the water as source of life) in the nothing disappears, then the universe disappears along with it.

When we apply these ideas to Freudian and Lacanian psychoanalysis, what do we get? Well, the Freudian repressed unconscious is kept repressed in a low state that appears not to exist (people say that the unconscious does not exist), and yet it does and constitutes an animate/inanimate bedrock for the psyche. The default state of nature is the void or vacuum, so the animate drives emerge from the inanimate. The Real unconscious, Lacan says, "ex-sists" or at least does not exist in the ordinary sense of the signifier. The Real unconscious can be a true hole or vacuum and exist outside matter and signification and at the same time give matter and signification its watermark, unary trace, or "jouissance structure".

The Symbolic makes a cut or hole in the Real in the sense that the world of real things is determined by the signifier, while the Real refers to a jouissance outside the signifier that also structures its internal relations. The Real also makes a cut or hole in the Symbolic because the Real, which structures the Symbolic order's internal relations, appears as something missing within the Symbolic. While the world seems determined by language, within language something "ex-sists" that is fundamental for the order of language and yet is found missing within language.

Returning to Freud's essay, he goes on to state that the constancy principle is

> only another way of stating the pleasure principle. . . . The pleasure principle follows from the principle of constancy: actually the latter principle was inferred from the facts which forced us to adopt the pleasure principle. Moreover, a more detailed discussion will show that the tendency which we thus attribute to the mental apparatus is subsumed as a special case under

---

1 Please see the link: www.askamathematician.com/2012/07/q-what-is-the-false-vacuum-and-are-we-living-in-it.

> Fechner's principle of the "tendency towards stability", to which he has brought the feelings of pleasure and unpleasure into relation.
>
> (Freud, 1920/1961, p. 3)

The constancy principle is another way to understand the dynamics of the pleasure principle. But this time, Freud goes on to discuss how the pleasure principle is replaced and opposed by forces such as the reality principle and the repetition compulsion. The pleasure principle persists as the traditional method of the sexual drive and of the repressed formations of the sexual drive. "The fulfillment of wishes is, as we know, brought about in a hallucinatory manner by dreams, and under the dominance of the pleasure principle this has become their function" (idem, p. 26). In turn, both the reality principle and the return of the repressed cause the experience of unpleasure. The compulsion to repeat is a subsequent force that will oppose the pleasure principle.

In analysis, repressed material is repeated in the transference instead of "remembered" (re-organized) from something belonging to the past. At the same time, what opposes the repressed is the conscious and unconscious ego of the analysand.

> There is no doubt that the resistance of the conscious and unconscious ego operates under the sway of the pleasure principle: it seeks to avoid the unpleasure which would be produced by the liberation of the repressed. Our efforts, on the other hand, are directed towards procuring the toleration of that unpleasure by an appeal to the reality principle.
>
> (idem, p. 14)

Here, the reality principle is located not in the ego but in the present agency of the analyst. While Freud initially says that the reality ego opposes the pleasure principle, here he asserts that both the repressed drives and repressive ego operate under the pleasure principle. He goes on further to state that the reality principle itself is a modification of the pleasure principle that does not abandon the aim of obtaining pleasure. Thus, when the ego tries to avoid unpleasure, it is trying to avoid unpleasure caused not only by the sexual drive and the return of the repressed but by the reality principle itself. Because the reality principle modifies the pleasure principle and redefines it in the context of acceptable pleasure within reality, the pleasure ego opposing the pleasure drive is the case of a previously modified pleasure principle under the reality principle. In this essay, a prior opposition between the reality principle and the more archaic pleasure principle at work within the drive results in a synthesis whereby the pleasure principle now serves the purposes of defending against the drives.

Now, we might ask how this formulation of the pleasure principle through the constancy principle bears on appreciating the Buddhist elements in Lacanian thought.

> "People who know the state of emptiness will always be able to dissolve problems by constancy." (Suzuki, 1974, p. 83) The usual translation of the

Japanese word *nin* is "patience," but perhaps "constancy" is a better word. You must force yourself to be patient, but in constancy there is no particular effort involved – there is only the unchanging ability to accept things as they are. For people who have no idea of emptiness, this ability may appear to be patience, but patience can actually be non-acceptance. People who know, even if only intuitively, the state of emptiness, always have open the possibility of accepting things as they are. In everything they do, even though it may be very difficult, they will always be able to dissolve their problems by constancy.

(idem, p. 86)

We cultivate the spirit with the way of continuous practice. Continuous practice is like living in the emptiness of the dark empty sky, witnessing lightning and beautiful sceneries, and then forgetting about it all. Lightning requires the tolerance of both charge and discharge, constancy, and Nirvana. We gather and retain knowledge on an ongoing basis and at the same time constantly clear our mind or forget all about knowledge from the point of view of the ego. Not that we clear our mind by being ignorant or not having any knowledge. In emptiness, there is always understanding. The Nirvana principle clears the mind, or leaves it empty, and without representation, which corresponds with the first layer of the perceptual conscious system. At the same time, such clearing facilitates the registration of representations in the back systems of the mind. A layer or level of mind evacuates perceptions according to the Nirvana principle, and other layers must tolerate the retention of excitations linked to memory and representation. Freud's Pcpt.-Cs. system does not retain any impressions or memories and represents the blank screen or the mystical writing pad. In this sense, we can say that pure awareness functions according to the discharge or non-retention of perceptual phenomena. The Pcs.-Cs. system and the Ucs. systems must tolerate and retain memories and perceptual phenomena with the help of the constancy principle.

The ego is an early object of the drive in the form of the ideal ego and the specular image that exists against the background of the empty mirror that Lacan proposes represents the emptiness or inexistence of the Other. The ideal ego stands in the place of the object of the drive. The ego first acquires a libidinal and bodily characteristic in relationship to the specular image, what we will discuss later in the book as the body image in the clear mirror.

But the specular image also represents the reality principle insofar as the specular image constitutes an attempt to cope with the separation from the mother and the object of the drive. Hence, the *objet a* is also ultimately absent from the image in the mirror. The *objet a* is represented by a blank spot or a hole in the image that makes the child turn toward the father's law and recognition, precipitating thereby, the transformation of the ideal ego into the ego ideal.

Once the ego ideal is established, the pleasure principle will be even further transformed and defined by the reality principle in terms of "the pleasure of the father's good values" rather than the good of pleasure associated with the archaic mother and the jouissance of the Other. The repressive principle introduced by the symbolic reality of the father appears to be a transformed pleasure principle (under the reality principle) differentiated from and turned against an earlier form of pleasure. Once repression and the ego ideal also work under the pleasure principle, the pleasure principle contains or has antinomian forces operating under its aegis.

If both drives and defenses work for the pleasure principle, what happens to the opposition between the pleasure principle and the reality principle? The opposition between these two principles is always rooted in a conventional definition of the pleasure principle as a form of hedonism. Freud's example is of the artist. However, when the reality principle transforms the pleasure principle with the acceptance of frustration, symbolic castration, and the inevitable postponements of satisfactions, how does this differ from the two aspects of the pleasure principle (drive and defense)?

The difference is that the acceptance of frustration/castration is a semi-conscious process, while repression and the work of the signifier under the pleasure principle is mostly unconscious. The operation of repression takes place within the unconscious structure of language and signification itself. Both the repressive and repressed unconscious work under the pleasure principle, while the reality principle opposes or at least can be distinguished from both.

For Lacan, what opposes the duality of the pleasure principle is the reality of the presence of the analyst. However, the presence of the analyst is not the same as the reality principle. The presence of the analyst offers the dimension of dialogue through which a subject is constituted as a subject. To be clear, the analyst does not represent the norms and standards of the Other. Lacan rejects the tendency to normalize the outcomes of analysis according to external social expectations. In this sense, objective and positive therapeutic outcomes are the same as those that comply with the norms of a standard analysis. Ideology and objective treatment outcomes mirror each other. Thus, to adopt so-called scientific prescriptions in analysis is an imaginary ideological effect of creating a complete subject and is not what Lacan would consider a scientific process.

How, then, might psychoanalysis be constituted as a science? What might a scientific position for the analyst be? In his *Ecrit* (2006c) "On the subject who is finally in question" (p. 193), Lacan asks about the similarity and difference between psychoanalysis and the transmission of knowledge that occurs through apprenticeship within a professional organization. Is the ideological effect of standardization and normalization the same as a professional training institution? In both apprenticeship and psychoanalysis, the transmission of truth and knowledge is personal, in contrast to the bureaucratic and impersonal truth and knowledge of the university or academic institution.

Yet the personal is not simply a more in-depth way to drive the structure of the Other and society into the subject. Given this, Lacan rejects the comparison between psychoanalysis and apprenticeship and asserts that analysis requires an entirely different position for the subject. He does this in part by differentiating the terms "master" and "teacher." In the West, the master is a social master who wields political power and often uses it to oppress those under his charge. This definition of a master is no different from that of a social ego or super-ego.

In Eastern traditions of Buddhism, like Chan and Zen, however, the notion of the master has a different meaning. The master is the One who has realized his or her own emptiness or own non-being. In a prior work, Moncayo has distinguished between an imaginary social master of One, and a master of none. The master of none is a One that includes zero or its own non-being. In this case, the imaginary egoic social master has been subjectively destituted in a good way. When the analyst functions out of the position of a social master, this threatens to derail a scientific and properly subjective transmission of psychoanalysis.

In other words, the scientific position of the analyst is achieved through a use and a suspension of the position of the analyst as subject supposed to know. The analyst functions in a position of *savior* rather than a completed or packaged knowledge. *Savior* here is deployed to help articulate the subject's desire in speech rather than tell the subject what his or her social desires should be.

However, in examining the subject's desire in analysis, the desire and lack of the Other is always considered. This is not to have the subject subordinate his or her desire to the other's desire, or primarily orient the subject toward satisfying the other's desire over the subject's own. Instead, the subject must recognize his or her own desire within a loop that includes the other's desire, and therein decide what he or she wants the desire to be. This consideration can and does exist in an apprenticeship relationship, like it does in the Chan teacher–student relationship. The teacher always gives back to the student what intrinsically belongs to him or her, rather than filling the student's mind with the teacher's ideas and beliefs. The desire for realization is articulated as an intrinsic desire of the student, rather than simply an attempt to imitate and identify with the social prestige or accomplishments of the teacher.

The imaginary wish to imitate and identify with the social prestige of the teacher results in imaginary identifications that reproduce the teacher's ego rather than his or her inner realization. The similarity and difference between imaginary identifications within Samsara or ego experience and symbolic identifications that transmit something Real or Nirvanic within experience offers a valuable perspective on Freud's discussion of the repetition compulsion, and Lacan's differentiation between automaton and Tyche as two principles of accidental causality or chance. In automaton, the teacher takes something from the student for his or her own ego, or the student identifies with the teacher's ego rather than the pure signifiers associated with the teaching. In Tyche's case, surprises and accidental events predispose the subject toward enlightening experiences beyond the ego. That is, the analyst, understood in the spirit of Chan, gives the analysand back what intrinsically belongs to him or her in the form of the emptiness of desire, and the drive as the default vacuum state. The subject here is recognized both as a metaphor and as an It-subject, or a subject in the Real, rather than as an ego or an ego-Id formation.

According to Freud, the compulsion to repeat is made up of (1) new attempts at unconsciously satisfying previously denied desires and impulses that a subject does not take responsibility for; and (2) an infantile sexuality that could never be satisfied in the past (due to the incest prohibition and the physical limitations of the child and the demands of reality across time). An example of this would be a woman who must be abandoned by all her partners because the partner uncon-sciously represents the father. Because an impulse was in fact satisfied in child-hood and she won her father (whether figuratively or literally), she is condemned to lose him in the future. Such a woman unconsciously forces herself to pay for having triumphed over the mother in childhood.

Freud also discusses the repetition compulsion as passive experiences of suffer-ing over which an individual has no overt control and that therefore seems to be fated. This is given in his discussion of the example of a woman who experienced the successive deaths of three husbands. Freud finds in experiences provided by traumas and traumatic neurosis the clearest example of how a repetition compul-sion does not work under the sway of the pleasure principle since it yields pain more than pleasure or relaxation. This formulation of the pleasure principle (as the tendency to avoid unpleasure) cannot limit the suffering linked to the repetition compulsion or the pleasure associated with forbidden satisfactions. It is here that Freud comes to formulate a function more fundamental than the pleasure principle. Such a function is the "beyond" of the pleasure principle regulating archaic wishes and tendencies, as well as beyond the pleasure principle at work in unconscious repression.

> The fulfillment of wishes is, as we know, brought about in a hallucinatory manner by dreams, and under the dominance of the pleasure principle this has become their function. But it is not in the service of that principle that the dreams of patients suffering from traumatic neurosis lead them back with such regularity to the situation in which the trauma occurred.
>
> (Freud, 1920, p. 26)

Anxiety dreams or punishment dreams do not constitute exceptions to the pleasure principle,

> for they merely replace the forbidden wish-fulfillment by the appropriate punishment for it; that is to say, they fulfill the wish of the sense of guilt which is the reaction to the repudiated impulse.
>
> (idem)

Freud suggests that punishment dreams are the consequence of a deadliness within the unconscious ego or super-ego as an indirect result of the prohibition of incest (the Symbolic in Lacan's work). And although punishment dreams or the compulsion to repeat, and the related wish for guilt and punishment, still demon-strate the existence of an earlier and more archaic wish for which the ego needs to be punished by the super-ego, they also demonstrate the wish to experience unpleasure or pain rather than pleasure. This is demonstrated in the previously discussed example of the pain of losing or of being left and abandoned.

While such punishment dreams may represent pain for the ego and for the repressed drive, they also represent pleasure or satisfaction for the punitive agency.

For this reason, and because of the existence of an earlier repudiated impulse, Freud concludes that punishment dreams do not constitute an exception to the pleasure principle. Pleasure in pain, as a masochistic phenomenon, can be understood as pleasure for the super-ego but pain for the ego and for the drive.

If punishment dreams are not exceptions to the pleasure principle, traumatic dreams also are not exceptions to the pleasure principle, but for different reasons. In the case of traumatic dreams, the compulsion to repeat is "helping to carry out another task, which must be accomplished before the dominance of the pleasure principle can even begin" (idem). Freud identifies this prior task with the task of binding the primary process of freely mobile cathexis with the bound energy that characterizes the secondary process. The important point here is that the task of binding excitation has precedence over the pleasure principle defined as a principle of immediate discharge and total evacuation. However, it is unclear how this task would be different from a pleasure principle already modified in the service of mental defenses. It is also unclear how this task is primary given that Freud otherwise considers the task of binding excitation as a secondary and not a primary process.

Perhaps Freud could not clarify these points and terms because he was using insufficient physiological terminology on energy and constancy borrowed from Breuer and Helmholtz. Constancy for Breuer constituted the homeostasis of a specialized central nervous system, while Freud assumes the circulation of free energy. Breuer distinguished between two forms of energy – quiescent and kinetic energy, which both circulate throughout the nervous system. For Breuer, the purpose of achieving an optimal level of regulating tension is the free circulation of kinetic energy, which results in an easy functioning of thought, and the existence of unblocked or unhindered associations. In other words, a base level of constancy coincides with a state of health and symbolic free association. Clarity of mind, for example, corresponds with an optimal level of tonic energy in which energy circulates proportionally from representation to representation. For Breuer, the energy of dreams and the primary process could not be free because of a decline of a basic tonic potential (Moncayo, 1997, p.128).

Freud strikingly reversed the primary and secondary functions of Breuer's two energies: "again it is easy to identify the primary psychical process with Breuer's freely mobile cathexis and the secondary process with changes in his bound or tonic cathexis" (Freud, 1920, p. 28). To Breuer, the free (mobile) circulation of kinetic energy is a *secondary* function of the *primary* need to establish an optimum base level of quiescent energy. In contrast, one encounters Freud's version of the primary process when what Breuer sees as the primary function of obtaining a basic tonic level fails. Freud inverts the relationship that Breuer established between quiescent tonic energy and the free circulation of kinetic energy (Moncayo, 1997, p. 129). Nevertheless, in *Beyond the Pleasure Principle*, Freud seems to find his way back to defining the binding of the primary process under the pleasure principle as a primary and original task. By saying that the secondary process is the earliest and most important function, Freud suggests that it is a primary and original function.

The idea of defining pleasure as an optimal bound tension is also implied two years later in "The Economic Problem of Masochism" (Freud, 1924). In this paper, Freud wrote that there could be pleasurable increases of tension and unpleasant decreases of tension. Since for the most part, human beings find sexual excitation rather enjoyable, it seemed more reasonable to attribute pleasure to a tendency to establish an optimal level of tension and keep it constant (Moncayo, 1997, p. 125). This would be consistent with the earlier quote, in which Freud comes to regard pleasure as a function of the constancy principle. "The pleasure principle follows from the principle of constancy: actually the latter principle was inferred from the facts which forced us to adopt the pleasure principle" (Freud, 1920, p. 3).

The constancy principle is also reflected in Lacan's statement that the fundamental ethical decision is to take responsibility for one's desire. Taking responsibility for desire cannot be reduced to repression or acting out. Both acting out and repression are ruled out by the Nirvana principle defined as a tendency to completely evacuate all excitations. Constancy represents acceptance rather than the repression of desire. Acceptance, or the recognition of desire, and the recognition of the ego's desire for recognition, also involves not acting on desire without prior deliberation or choice.

Deliberation, choice, and responsibility all require the tolerance of fresh tensions introduced by the desire for recognition and the recognition of desire. Even the existence of the unconscious requires that tensions and unpleasure be tolerated in the back systems of the mind. Only the front layer/level of the mind or the Pcpt.-Cs. system does not retain any impressions so that new impressions may be received. Therefore, Lacan says that the Freudian unconscious is a false hole because it only appears to be a black hole or box with nothing in it, when in fact, important conflictual material has lodged itself there, resisting therefore the push for a complete evacuation or Nirvanic emptying out. Unconscious psychical structure already has a need for tolerating unpleasant representations beyond what the conscious subject may need to accept to function in the world. Only the Real unconscious represents a box without a lid and whose bottom has fallen out. The Real unconscious is outside any signifying box.

Since for the most part, human beings find sexual excitation rather enjoyable, up to the point where pleasure turns into pain. The law and the prohibition of sexual pleasure itself is a form of pleasure so prohibition can also be used for sexual purposes. Subjects can only deviate from their social responsibilities on a temporary basis and otherwise have to maintain the asexual energy constant. The idea of defining pleasure as an optimal bound tension is also implied two years later in "The Economic Problem of Masochism" (Freud, 1924). In this paper, Freud wrote that there could be pleasurable increases of tension and unpleasant decreases of tension.

Surveying how these relationships change across Freud's work, we can see now that his various formulations all depend on how he poses the question of the "beyond" of the pleasure principle by testing and critiquing existing concepts of the latter. It is the definition of the pleasure principle that determines the definitions of the other principles. At the same time, Freud seems to conclude that the constancy principle opposes the pleasure principle insofar as the latter is understood as constituted by a hallucinatory form of wish fulfillment.

In seeking to understand the "beyond" of the pleasure principle, Freud succeeded in reversing the definition of the Nirvana principle that he borrowed from Buddhism in a similar way he reversed Breuer's constancy principle. For Buddhism, Nirvana is a bound state in which energy flows freely like a mountain stream flowing in the dark of night. The flow of the stream is shaped by the surface structure of the mountain.

Buddhism considers the hallucinatory pursuits of ego-clinging or clinging to the objects of desire, a form of delusion or mistaken enlightenment, where the subject is neither free nor satisfied. In contrast, Freud seems to regard Nirvana as a form of satisfaction of the object of desire, which is, even according to his own thought, impossible. His reference to Nirvana seems to suggest that heaven, or paradise, could be represented by fusion with the maternal object. While it is understandable that people might read Freud's use of Nirvana as a form of archaic wish fulfillment, this is an incorrect interpretation, in part because this is not how Buddhism regards Nirvana, but as well, because it goes against Freud's own discussion of the constancy principle.

Freud differentiates the constancy principle as a mode of binding excitation from the pleasure principle. He does this by questioning whether bound or quiescent energy involves retaining an optimal level of tension/energy or discharging it altogether. For example, he speaks of the "most universal endeavor of all living substance – namely to return to the quiescence of the inorganic world" (idem, p. 56). Here, quiescence appears as a final state, while he also states that quiescence is a "preliminary function designed to prepare the excitation for its final elimination in the pleasure of discharge" (idem).

Freud's references to the Nirvana principle and the constancy principle as ways to understand the "beyond" the pleasure principle represent a more fundamental question about whether pleasure is an absolute discharge or a constant or optimal level of energy. There is more than one way to skin the cat when it comes to posing the question of the "beyond" the pleasure principle.

Freud's conclusion, ultimately, is to define pleasure as both absolute discharge and constancy, where constancy is theorized somewhat independently from the magnitude (increase or decrease) and quality of the stimulus. Constancy here represents a sort of evenness or equanimity in the face of variations and changes in the quantity (rise and fall) and quality (pleasant or unpleasant) of the emotions, for example. Under constancy, pleasure is secured by preventing that pleasure from turning into unpleasure, and by placing a limit on the development of unpleasure. Constancy and pleasure represent a *variable* optimal level of tension beyond which unpleasure is generated.

Our reading of Freud on the pleasure and constancy principles aligns in some respects with Ricoeur's (1970). However, rather than following Ricoeur's phenomenological theory of discourse, we are ultimately interested in Freud's discussion of the constancy principle insofar as it allows us to extend both the Nirvana principle and constancy principle into an engagement with how Lacan preserves and re-signifies the polyvocal meanings of death within psychoanalysis.

How is death or the second death linked to the Symbolic order? Further, how is the Real linked to death, insofar as death remains something unknown, a form of bliss or agony beyond language? The second death within life, attributed to the Symbolic, is how the Symbolic can represent a gateless gate of access to the Real beyond symbolization. Something missing within the Symbolic points to something Real outside the Symbolic. In Chan, the second symbolic or spiritual death, or enlightenment as a death of the ego, revitalizes the metaphor of the subject, rather than killing the living body.

Nirvana as a second death is what sustains the Symbolic order by the establishment of a so-called false vacuum state that prevents the complete elimination of energy leading to death or the vanishing of both subject and universe alike. The ego vanishes before the signifier that speaks for the subject, and at the same time the signifier is a "spirit" or a sound without substantial material existence within the body-mind of the subject. The signifier has no physical presence other than as speech or writing. When we say the ego vanishes under the signifier, we are saying that the imaginary ego vanishes into the true vacuum, and that only the letter, and the spirit and soul of the word, remain in the constancy of the false vacuum that must be tolerated for the word and the world to exist.

Recall that when Freud speaks about the exceptions to the pleasure principle or what opposes the pleasure principle, he is in fact referring to archaic wish fulfillment and not to Breuer's primary function of binding excitation. The latter is what is beyond the former, that is, binding excitation is what is beyond archaic wish fulfillment. For Freud, binding excitation and optimal tension are more basic than archaic wish fulfillment under the pleasure principle.

Lacan, in turn, argues the reverse. What Freud then defined as the pleasure principle is a principle of constancy (1920/1965, p. 3). For Lacan, the pleasure principle is the constancy principle and what is beyond the pleasure principle is *jouissance*, defined as seeking pleasure, fantasy, or excessive hallucinatory wish fulfillment, or the death drive defined as a principle of complete discharge. Lacan (1954–1955) regards the pleasure principle as a principle of homeostasis and defines *jouissance as both pleasure and suffering* that goes beyond the pleasure principle.

The tendency to repeat is often associated with suffering and the tendency to repeat past trauma and conflicts.

> The compulsion to repeat would be beyond the pleasure principle. Since it would constitute the condition for a kind of human progress, instead of being, like the pleasure principle, a relation of security.
>
> (idem, p. 23)

How could the compulsion to repeat be a motor for human progress since it is always involved in the production of suffering and psychopathology? Only Tyche is the true form of chance that has a redemptive or progressive quality, but by Lacan's own understanding, Tyche must also be differentiated from automaton or the repetition compulsion. Lacan in the previous quote collapses the distinction between automaton and Tyche, only the latter of which refers to repetition as an opportunity to heal and do something different with the repetition. Only Tyche can be considered a condition for human progress.

Despite privileging the insecurity of the compulsion to repeat as a motor for human progress, Lacan was aware of the deadliness of trying to repeat destructive or inconvenient forms of jouissance, or of idealizing a principle of enjoyment outside the Law in the form of hallucinatory wish fulfillment. Instead, Lacan's work provides a platform to think about jouissance in different ways (he defined three types of jouissance), including thinking about optimal tension or quiescence as a form of jouissance. By foregrounding our Chan Buddhist informed reading of Freud's text, this Lacanian critique is further supported by a notion of constancy understood without the classical or conventional notion of ego and in the direction of Lacan's third Other jouissance.

Chapter 5

Wu and Mu in the *Cáodòng zōng* and *Línjì* Schools

Since Lacan believed that the sexual drive was linked to the unconscious through the nodal point of desire, we can also approach the paradoxical nature of the drive reflected on the surface of the question of desire. Desire in turn depends on sexual demands articulated in language that always leave an unsatisfied, metonymic remainder running under them (Lacan, 1964/1981, p. 154). Desire remains in-between signifiers since demand cannot extinguish the tensions associated with desire and the signifiers of sexual demand. And because the pressure of the drive is interchangeable with the demands of the Other or the jouissance of the Other, the social Other is often identified in the Imaginary as the pressures of the biological drive. The object of the reproductive and biological sexual drive becomes an object cause of desire, or the *objet a*, ruled by signifiers, but filtered by the tension between Symbolic and Imaginary identifications with the social Other.

> You have heard speak, I think, if only in Freud, about the reference to Nirvana. I think that you may have here and there heard speak of it in such a fashion that you could not identify it to a pure reduction to nothingness. The very usage of negation which is current in Zen for example, and the recourse to the sign "Mu" which is that of negation here, should not deceive you, the sign "Mu" involved being moreover a very particular negation which is a "not to have."
>
> (Lacan, 08.05.63 XVII 154)

The term *Mu*, referenced by Lacan here, comes from Japanese (無) and Korean (Hanja: 無; or Hangul: 무). The term is also found in Chinese as *Wu* (traditional Chinese: 無; simplified Chinese: 无), also meaning "not have," "without," or "lack." These are key words in Buddhism, especially in the Chan and Zen traditions but also for Lacanian psychoanalysis. Given that Chan or Zen Buddhism is considered a hybrid of Buddhism, Taoism, and Confucianism, the meaning of the word in Chinese Taoism, *Wuwei*, as developed by *Lao Tse* (500–400 BC) in the *Tao Te Ching*, and later developed by his disciple, *Chuang Tzu* (369–286 BC), in *The Way of Chuang Tzu*, is important for us to consider. *Wuwei* can mean either

DOI: 10.4324/9781003198765-5

non-doing as in "nothing is done and yet everything gets accomplished in silence" or as "the value of restraint of overt aggressiveness in individual striving." As Batchelor observes, "*Chuang Tzu* agrees with the Buddha that emptiness entails an absence of a solid self that is realized through meditation discipline (which was present in Hinduism). Yet *Chuang Tzu* presents emptiness as a playful, anarchic freedom unconstrained by religiosity."

Wuwei could also be translated as the value of restraint of overt aggressiveness and competitiveness in individual striving. Such "know-how," praxis, or *savior* is a form of transmission and realized activity. Nothing is done from the point of view of profit or gaining idea, and yet everything gets accomplished. Productivity is based on emptiness, which is the source of the drives. Wu in Buddhism represents a pure human awareness, prior to having experience or knowledge. Moncayo (2018) has argued that this pure awareness in psychoanalysis represents Freud's Pcpt.-Cs. system that receives all the data from the senses but does not retain any memories, representations, or impressions. The latter takes place in systems behind it: the Ucs.-Pcs. and the Pcs.-Cs systems. The "original nonbeing" from which being is produced is a negative, a form of nonexistence or inexistence, something impossible, lacking reason or cause. Thus, the Mu we encounter in Lacan's discourse carries a "very particular negation" of "not to have": a nonexistence, non-being, not having, a lack of, or "being without" that is also everything everywhere.

This sense of Wu appears in the Chan story we discuss later. It can be found in the two collections of koans compiled by the two main schools of Zen: Soto and Rinzai in Japanese, or *Cáodòng zōng* and *Línjì* in Chinese. A koan is a public case or dialogue in which the maturity or understanding of the student is tested. The koan that refers to Mu appears as Case 18 of the Book of Serenity (Cleary, 2005) of the Soto school, or Case 1 of the Gateless Barrier of the Rinzai school (*Wu-men kuan: Mumonkan*, Aitken, 1990). Customarily traced back in Chinese history to the late fifth and early sixth centuries CE, the dramatic culmination of Chan Zen literature took place during the tenth and 13th centuries.

The Book of Serenity (《从容录》) was compiled in China by the *Cáodòng* school (Chinese: 曹洞宗; pinyin: *Cáodòng zōng*). Its founder was *Dongshan Liangjie* (807–869, Japanese: *Tozan Ryokai*; Korean: *Tongsan Lianggye*). At the age of 52, *Dongshan* established a school at the mountain named *Dongshan* (in what is now the city of *Gao'an* in *Jiangxi* province). In our discussion below, due to the translation and commentary, we will use the Gateless Barrier of the Rinzai school.

The famous case of *Chao-chou*'s dog (赵州犬子 or Joshu's in Japanese) is as follows:

A monk asked, "Does a dog have a Buddha-nature or not?"
The master said, "Not [Mu]!"

The monk said, "Above to all the Buddhas, below to the crawling bugs, all have
  Buddha-nature. Why is it that the dog has not?"
The master said, "Because he has the nature of karmic delusions".

(Aitken, 1990, p. 7)

Because emptiness is beyond conceptualization, both positive and negative
answers are absurd because there is no thing called Buddha-nature. When the
teacher or a student is asked the question, they must ponder that if they say
"yes," they may lose their own Buddha-nature because the answer is not yes.
But if they say "no," do they also lose their Buddha-nature? No, because "no-
Buddha-nature," in this case, is not a mundane denial of Buddha-nature.

To better understand this, we might ask whether *Chao-chou*'s (Joshu's) "no"
is binary or unary. Binary negation represents a negation of something particular.
For example, I don't like a particular food. A binary negation in the Mu case would
mean that a dog has nothing to do with Buddha, or in other words, that the very
Aristotelian definition of a dog excludes it from being Buddha.

Unary negation, in contrast, does not deny any specific affirmation. It denies
that truth proper could be represented in any affirmative way as a theorem of T.
The positive is outside language, outside a "yes" or "no" answer, just as jouissance
lies outside the signifier. Mu or Wu in this koan operates as a unary negation.

Buddha-nature requires the unary negation of Mu because it refers to *das Ding*,
or the "no-thing" that is not a thing. To the question "Does a dog have Buddha-
nature?", on the one hand, the monk *Chao-chou* replied affirmatively (yes), but
when challenged by the Master with "Mu!", he reasoned that withholding an affirmative (yes) necessarily required accepting a negative (no): "Above to all the
Buddhas, below to the crawling bugs, all have Buddha-nature." Why is it that the
dog has not? This negation is similarly performed in ancient Greek philosophy.
Plato, for example, said that dogs have the soul of a philosopher. The pre-Socratic
philosopher Diogenes the cynic, however, referred to himself as a dog. He considered himself an object of waste (*a*) and lived inside a trash can.

For Diogenes, a human being is not a higher being than a dog because a dog has
the soul of a philosopher and not simply that of a human being. The dog as a philosopher or Buddha is more than a human being, rather than the dog being more
primitive than a human being as has been commonly believed. In the same way, a
lower object of waste, or the *objet a*, is privileged over other common objects. As
an object of waste, the philosopher becomes something precious and exalted. The
objet a is a jewel found inside a heap of waste.

The cultural background and context for the koan is often left out in many
accounts, just as the origin of "*gong'an*" or "koan" dialogues in Asian literary
games is also left out. The historical Shakyamuni Buddha eliminated the Hindu
caste system within Buddhist communities. However, Confucian Chinese society
was rank ordered and stratified. Just as there are differences among peoples of
various ranks, there is a rank order between animals and humans, not unlike how
humans are given dominion over animals in the Bible. That Buddha said all beings

are the Buddha-nature must be interpreted within these historically varying contexts to properly understand and convey that if we interpret the answer to the koan as a binary and conventional no, then we fail to recognize the enlightened nature of animals who also follow and teach the treasure of the true law within their species being. Animals eat each other, but when fed, they ordinarily do not and can be very tender and loving toward their caretakers, whom they also care for.

We believe that Lacan's allusion to Mu or Wu as a "very particular negation" resonates most with the Soto (*Cáodòng*) School approach to Zen meditation as a practice of silent illumination and "themeless breath-awareness" in the body that uses koans as teaching devices. This contrasts with the Rinzai (*Línjì*) School, which emphasizes focusing/thinking on a koan during meditation. Notably, neither Shakyamuni nor Nagarjuna adopted or recommended this form of thinking. This is not to say, however, that productive thinking cannot take place in "*zuo Chan*" (zazen) and, therefore, thinking of a koan might be an improved practice over ordinary thinking. Still, many of the Rinzai commentaries on this koan about the Buddha-nature of the dog emphasize an exclusive concentration on the "head word" or master signifier Wu. Through such concentration, one is admonished from knowing Wu in terms of "has" or "has not," rather than being persuaded by the knowledge that Wu is not nothingness. The *Línjì* teacher becomes a naysayer: "Not this, not that," followed by the question: "What is it"? (它是什么? *Tā shì shénme?*) or "What is This"? (这是什么 Zhè shì shénme?). What is the Buddha-nature in the human: something human, animate, or inanimate? Notice that we did not include something divine so that the question can remain a purely natural or scientific question.

Clearly, Buddha-nature in humans includes compassion, although animals also have a capacity for compassion. In general, humans also consider compassion as what makes a person more rather than less human. As a metaphor, Buddha represents a rock or a foundation for a human being. In addition, Buddha is also included in nature, in rock and pebbles, in a way that humans may not be. But what does Lacan mean when he says that the subject is determined by symbolic chains of inanimate matter? Is the signifier animate or inanimate, living, or dead, and does this mean that Buddha or Nirvana is something inanimate within human beings? But then how could the flowers of compassion grow out of lifeless inanimate rocks? These are all the paradoxical questions associated with the Wu *gong'an*.

Ultimately, whatever answer may be given is not "It." Through query, admonition, and naysaying, the expectation is that the answer will come from deep within the subject of the Real once the intellect has been taken away.

Indeed, the writings of Dogen Zenji in Japan were critical of anti-intellectual yelling and slapping in the *Línjì* or Rinzai school, which lies at a point of maximum conflict with Western rationality and science. This, of course, is not to deny that the intellect could also be harmful to human beings or cover over and impede Buddha-nature. However, the tension between these two points of view is precisely the narrow path that *Cáodòng* Chan and Dogen traverse and goes beyond.

Koan practice in the *Línjì* or Rinzai school can lead to the illusion that the teacher has the answer to the koan since in his or her training, he or she had to have successfully passed through many, if not all, koans. However, the teacher does not have the answer for the student. Koan study with a teacher is a process wherein the student is repeatedly frustrated by the teacher's "no" or "not this or that." This "no" or the symbolic castration of the intellect, is what Lacan's calls *connaissance* (discriminating knowledge) rather than *savior* (knowing).

Savior is left in French to distinguish it from the more religious and philosophical term for wisdom. We understand that *savior* is generated by the strategic symbolic castration of the analytical intellect that can lead to a jouissance linked to the wisdom of emptiness. *Savior* is what comes from the Real without the interference of the intellect, reaching, thereby, a radical improvement and illumination of the intellect originally unknown to the subject. The teacher just says "no" to everything the student says, and it is *this* "no," more than the prior knowledge or experience of the teacher, that generates the answer to the koan within the student.

Wu-Men's classical *Línjì* (Rinzai) commentary warns us further that:

> For the practice of Zen it is imperative that you pass through the barrier set up by the Ancestral Teachers. When you pass through this barrier, you will not only interview *Chao-chou* intimately, but you will also walk hand in hand with all the Ancestral Teachers in the successive generations of our lineage.
>
> (Aitken, 1990, p. 7)

Intimacy requires a subjective and bodily transformation beyond language, a subjective awakening, rather than simply a form of intellectual understanding that keeps subjects external to one another.

From a Lacanian point of view, the barrier that needs to be traversed is the barrier of packaged knowledge as a basis for understanding. The barrier of knowledge refers to *connaissance* (discursive and unequivocal discriminating knowledge) or the attempt to gain enlightenment as an intellectual idea, or an idea of self-improvement. Both the things that need to be improved, and the ideas or reified concepts of improvement, or enlightenment, taken together stupefy or act as barriers for the subject.

To cross the barrier leading to intimacy with the teacher means to cross the barrier of ego ideals of enlightenment, or of ideal enlightened egos, as well as the barriers constituted by the subject's own problems, fantasies, and ways of constituting "What" is taking place in the practice and between teacher and student. Such intimacy in psychoanalysis is realized not as an imaginary oneness or fusion with the mother, but as a Real trans-subjective form of jouissance facilitated by the signifier and shared by analyst and analysand. When the signifier separates the "*i*" of the ego of the analysand involved in the fantasies about the Other, from the *a* [i (*a*)], then the *objet a* represents the Third jouissance that circulates between analyst and analysand.

The separation from the imaginary mother, and from the imaginary ego buttressed by the fantasy, leads to an *"accord du corps"* (a bodily accord) with the signifier, and eventually to a form of experience in the Real beyond the signifier. The gate of knowing is gateless, or *savior* is a clarity or a clear basis, because the S_1 delinked from the S_2 of packaged knowledge, and the *i* separated from the imaginary *objet a*, leads to non-packaged and senseless uses of the signifier in relationship to the Real of jouissance that now become commensurate to one another. The signifier or the gate is gateless in this case because it does not block access to the Third jouissance. Later, we will further examine the meaning of how the Real functions as an impossible barrier or obstacle for the subject. Such a barrier represents a test that furthers the maturity and *savior* of a subject.

Lacan defines Mu or Wu as "not-having," which is something the Rinzai teachers explicitly told us not to do. At the same time, Dogen's teaching, as the culmination of the Mahayana teaching and the Soto school in Japan, and in the East in general, clarified that all beings "are the Buddha-Nature." Rather than having it or not having it, beings are the Buddha-nature. But lest the "being the Buddha-nature" become something, or a thing, Being has to be understood as being the same as the One's own non-being. Buddha-nature is the same as "No Buddha-Nature." Buddha-nature *is* the vacuum rather than a positive being or material determination within the Imaginary or Symbolic.

The vacuum or emptiness is something. But what is this something? In terms of practice, "Not having" in Mu or Wu means no gaining idea or no aggressivity in striving, or productive activity or *savior* for its own sake: the love of Sophia or *savior*, the most effective aspect of analytic practice. However, since animal instincts arose from the void, dogs also are the Buddhaic nature of the void. Are dogs base, instinctual, and deluded or subhuman animals, while humans are noble? Or are we underestimating the nobility of animals? Since the Wu teaching of the Buddha is that all beings are noble or empty, dogs and cats also have nobility. Bodhisattvas (defined later) ride in accord with lions and elephants without taming or harming them.

Chapter 6

"No Buddha-Nature" and Buddha's Desire

The void is both Buddha-nature and "No Buddha-nature" because "No Buddha-nature" is Buddha-nature. *Guishan Lingyou* (沩山灵祐, *Kuei-shan Ling-yu, Isan Reiyu*, 771–853 CE), a descendant of *Mazu Daoyi* (马祖道一, 709–788) from *Dagui shan*, also called *Weishan Lingyou* (沩山灵祐) and *Daiwei* (*Daigu*), told his assembly in a simple logical symbolic statement, "All sentient beings have no Buddha-nature." This became a pivotal teaching of Dogen's Zen. "All sentient beings have no Buddha-nature" stands high as the crown jewel of the Buddha Way in China.

The question of the "Buddhaic" nature of the void, and of the Third jouissance in Lacan, raises the question of Buddha's desire and how desire differs from jouissance, as well as how ordinary human desire differs from the desire of the analyst. Can there be such a thing as Buddha's desire if, in the early sutras, Buddha states that Nirvana and enlightenment represent the extinction of desire?

The *Cáodòng*/Soto School considers the *Línjì*/Rinzai ideal of aggressively gaining or "attaining" enlightenment to be unrefined, primitive, or dualistic. Soto Zen regards attempts to "gain" enlightenment as tainted because such attempts presuppose that practice and enlightenment are distinct from each other.

Suzuki Roshi of the contemporary Soto school spoke of "practice-enlightenment" as the intimate concern of human activity or Buddha's desire. Buddha's desire is directed at the praxis of meditation instead of attaining enlightenment, since enlightenment is already there in practice. Turning and returning around the Real hole of *das Ding* or the "no-thing" is the backward step that turns and kindles the inward light. However, you and *zuo Chan* (Chan meditation), subject and *objet a* in the second Real, are not two different things. The *objet a* is more in you than you. *Zuo Chan* and everyday praxis are not two different things, either. Enlightenment is an inherent characteristic of human activity, but without practicing, we do not see or realize it.

The intention linked to "aspiration" and inspiration toward personal knowing – that which is "extimate" to the ego as a form of jouissance – differs from the intention associated with human desire for imaginary recognition and meaning (Lacan, 1960, p. 15). Aspiration and inspiration, the soul or jouissance of the word, instead represent Truth as a form of jouissance in the Real. For Buddha's desire, there is no contradiction between Buddha's desire and the Third jouissance. Buddha's desire partakes of the ordinary human desire as a lack or emptiness, stopping short of a full or fusional Imaginary jouissance with the Other.

DOI: 10.4324/9781003198765-6

The Third jouissance has already gone through the emptying and nullification of the phallic function of symbolic castration that generates the inexistence of the imaginary phallus as a signifier of jouissance. The symbolic phallus instead appears in the place of the null set in set theory ($\varnothing \rightarrow \Phi$). The signifier of jouissance appears out of the vacuum, or as signifier of emptiness, if emptiness had a One that is a zero or a cipher, much like the Sanskrit Lingam as the abstract form of the formless Shiva.

In his introduction to the Seminar on the Names of the Father, Lacan (1963) addresses the Judeo-Christian tradition not unlike how he speaks of the voice of YHVH ("Yahweh" for many non-Jewish translators) we find in section XVIII of the Seminar on Anxiety under consideration. The voice of YHVH, just like the shout of the Zen/Chan teacher, and the sound of the Jewish *shofar* (ram's horn), represents the lion's roar or the voice as an *objet a*, index, or sign of the realm (Real). Here again, the voice, rather than the content of speech, represents the jouissance outside or in-between speech.

To be consistent with Lacanian theory and the Torah, the common name "Lord" should be rendered as YHVH. The consonants need to be placed more as a string of numbers or knots rather than letters with vowels. And the terrifying face of YHVH, or the divine *terribilita*, not to be confused with Lacan's first acceptation of the Real, is linked to the voice and the shout more than the word. The voice as an *objet a* is also linked to the *objet a* that the One desire demands from the subject and from the community of citizens as part of their social obligations and responsibilities.

For Lacan, G-d (God without o, the *objet a*) wants the foreskin of the phallus of the subject as a signifier of the Law and the covenant. G-d (structure, or the rules of the order) wants the subject to lose something, as in the phallic function of symbolic castration. That which the subject loses could also be the placenta, or the mother's breast. Freudian wish fulfillment, in this case, refers to fulfilling the Other's desire for the Law, and which Lacan restates as "The desire of the Other has taken the form of a command" (Lacan, 1962–1963, p. 277).

However, interpreting the appearance of YHVH in Lacan's teachings topologically, we must note that the notion of G-d's desire is staged in a Biblical story used to educate male and female children, and eventually, to make men and women, husbands and wives, out of them. In other words, the story is a myth, which interpreted topologically, also conveys something of the Real. In its strictest sense, the loss of the *objet a*, or the inexistence of the object of desire, is an effect of the operation of a mathematical structure (Φ-φ or $1.618 - 0.618 = i$ or 1), in contrast to what Feuerbach (1841) refers to as a human projection seen in an early modern notion of G-d's or the Other's desire. The human subject wants to be chosen and ordered to do the things that otherwise they are not inclined to do.

Even though we tend to regard sensitivity to the Other's desire, or the desire to fulfill the Other's desire, as a sign of ethical virtue, it is nonetheless ethically problematic. While the desire for the Other's desire, or a desire for the Law, has obvious social advantages and utilities, it is also what produces the conditions for neurosis and the subject's alienation of his or her desire in the Other. Lacan could not articulate the modern challenge to the traditional ethic better than when he defines existential guilt this way: "The only thing one can be guilty of is giving ground relative to one's desire" (Lacan, 1959–1960, p. 321).

Herein lies a radical conflict between traditional culture and modern psycho-analysis. Traditional culture defines the subject's speech surrounding personal desires and demands as unjust, or unfair to the Other's desire. Therefore, the moral subject is expected to suppress his or her desires. In turn, when faced with a tra-ditional moral Other, the subject is expected to guess what the Other really wants and provide it as a form of service since the traditional Other only makes demands based on normative expectations and not on their inmost desires. The Other cannot have personal desires because the Other upholds the teaching that personal desires are "unjust." The Other does not make personal demands on a subject.

On the one hand, on the side of the subject, psychoanalysis conflicts with tradi-tional culture because the therapeutic method of free association allows the sub-ject to speak about his or her personal desires. On the other hand, on the side of the Other, the analyst differs from the traditional Other by allowing the subject to speak freely about his or her desire, but also shares with the traditional Other the nondisclosure of the analyst's personal desires to the analysand.

The subject has to take the analyst's desire as a given, where it either functions as the source of a fantasy of the subject about the Other's desire, or functions as an ambiguous source of meaning without words, of signifiers without signifieds. In having to guess the Other's desire, the subject is led to bring forth the fundamental questions of life and death, jouissance and signification. This is what Dogen called "*Osaku-sendaba*," where *sendaba* represents what the world seeks from each one of us and we bring forth whatever we deem to be *sendaba* or the most important in life.

In the practice of analysis, an analyst may indeed "divine" what the Other or the analysand wants, or what the Other's unconscious desire may be, but the point of the entire exercise is for the subject's desire to see the light of speech. Of course, that the subject can own what he or she wants does not mean that he or she must act on his or her desire. A subject may in fact decide that what he or she uncon-sciously wants is not what he or she really wants, is not his or her most intimate concern, or in his or her best interest or those of others.

Lacan also tells us that the lack in the Other means that there is no Other or Other behind the Other. Instead, there is a lack, or simply emptiness. Energetic sparks that began in the void (from negative charges to positive charges) grow into a human being that then either asks emptiness to tell him or her what to do, or projects and turns emptiness into immaterial objects of fantasy that color the perception of the other. Humans turn emptiness into a master, or emptiness turns humans into masters. Now, of course, it is also true that many believe that humans enslave themselves by turning what is "no-thing" into a deity or a sadistic task master. Therefore, then, it is also better, in any case, that the One function as emptiness or the One's own non-being, rather than risk being seen as a cruel and sadistic task master.

Chapter 7

The Vacuum in Western Science

The teaching that dogs "are the Buddha-nature" (emptiness) implies that animal instincts arose from the void. This view departs from an Aristotelian view that a vacuum is always filled with air because the universe does not allow a vacuum of empty space to be created without something that fills it. The common modern phrasing, "nature abhors a vacuum," comes from Rabelais in the 16th century, who summarized Aristotle's idea as "*natura abhorret vacuum*." However, if we look at Aristotle's Physics (IV 6–9), we find only his discussion of why vacuums are vacuous.

Aristotle's was the prevailing belief from 300 BC until Torricelli (1600; West, 2013, pp. 66–73) created empty space. Torricelli had succeeded in creating empty space without air between the bottom of the tube (turned upside down) and the line in the tube where the mercury stopped descending. With Torricelli's invention of the barometer, scientific experimentation revealed we live at the bottom of an ocean of air.

Pascal (1623 CE) would then show that air thins out the higher you go. Nothing is everywhere. The earth floats in the void. In fact, contrary to Rabelais's misleading aphorism, modern science reveals that nature does not abhor a vacuum. A vacuum is nature default's state. Here we see a continuity not between modern physics and Aristotelian thought, but between modern physics and Eastern thought, as represented by our previous discussion of Buddha-nature (Dogen, 1998b).

The importance of the scientific discovery of the vacuum can be seen in more recent technological innovations, as well. In 1887, Michelson determined that light moves through empty space, that the vacuum is empty and there is no ether. The vacuum became big business in the 20th century. From the light bulb to the TV, industry was able to make money out of nothing. Bulbs contain small volumes of nothing. The light bulb is light in the vacuum. The vacuum is the fundamental nature of reality. X-rays, the electron, and the atom were all discovered, thanks to the vacuum.

For the most part, quantum mechanics has only been able to approach the question of matter based on probability, and thus, uncertainty. It has proceeded by assuming that it is impossible to know the precise location and momentum of a

DOI: 10.4324/9781003198765-7

particle orbiting around the nucleus of an atom and uses statistical methods as the only way to calculate some indication of the location and momentum of a particle within its orbit. However, more recently, physicists are moving away from probabilistic analysis and considering the hypothesis that particles are dark matter.

This brings us back to the phenomenon of the vacuum, which is alive and contains energy waves (quantum fluctuations) that create particles out of emptiness. In tiny amounts of time and space, something can come from nothing. Theoretical physicist, Paul Dirac (1928), was a person of few words and preferred to work in silence. Dirac's principle of 'small enough but fast enough' united both the special theory of relativity and quantum mechanics. Dirac used matrix mathematics made of 0, 1, −1, and then he added i and -i (imaginary numbers), which allowed new particles to be discovered. A matrix is a group of numbers arranged in columns and rows. There are a certain number of combinations for these numbers inside the matrix. Lacan was particularly interested in the golden ratio as a particular set of numbers that emerge in binary matrixes. The new part of Dirac's equation containing imaginary numbers yielded antiparticles.

Things and anti-things annihilate, or cancel each other out, and turn into energy. Matter is created out of the energetic default state of the vacuum and then disappears back into energy, the same way that jouissance, as an energetic default state, represents the spray or glue of structure that appears and disappears from the chain of signifiers and organizes their relations. Emptiness is a seething mass of virtual particles that create turbulence for the electron orbit. The universe sprang from the vacuum as a fluctuation that shaped everything. The big bang produced equal amounts of matter and antimatter, but as the universe cooled down, + and − particles annihilated each other, albeit incompletely. For there is always a + 1 of matter left. Everything comes from this residual +1 of matter. From emptiness to infinity, this energy in the vacuum is the deepest of mysteries.

Chapter 8

Lacan and Wu

Lacan defines Wu (Mu in Korean and Japanese) or emptiness as "not having." Rather than merely an intellectual idea, not having in Mu or Wu means no gaining idea or no aggressivity in striving. Mu or Wu is not merely the absence of something but also connotes an approach to productive activity as *savior* for its own sake. "To say that desire is illusion is to say that it has no support, that it has no outcome in, nor aim towards anything" (Lacan, 08.05.63 XVII 154). We should now be able to clearly hear Lacan's quote as an interpretation of Wu. Wu as striving without imaginary aggressivity or ego ambition is more helpful than the Rinzai approach of simply denying the intellect completely. The latter act can lead to an infertile, or dead, stereotypical form of nothingness that is not Wu or emptiness.

We have discussed Nirvana as a term Freud (1920) adopted to represent a radical extinction of desire. Nirvana for Freud is a radical reduction of excitations to level zero, or a form of annihilation under the death drive. This principle or death drive, in his view, had to be modified or actualized in the form of a constant as the lowest form of tension needed to maintain the existence of mental structure. Combining our analysis of Nirvana, constancy, and Wu, with our previously elaborated discussion of the vacuum in theoretical physics, we now turn to a closer reading of the specific form of non-dualistic emptiness – Wu or Mu – present in both desire and Nirvana. Indeed, Lacan notes that "What is involved, at least in the median step of the relation to Nirvana, is always articulated, in a way that is spread throughout each and every formulation of Buddhist truth, in the sense of a non-dualism" (Lacan, 1962–1963, p. 223).

While terms such as desire, Nirvana, and constancy might sound abstract, when understood as forms of Wu or Mu, examples of concrete human experiences spring to mind. For example, aggressivity within striving involves rivalry and competition with others, predicated by the self-other duality. However, beyond rivalry and competition, striving as Wu or Mu is a way of speaking about being driven, or of a drive as a fundamental form of human activity. Work productivity and creativity arise from emptiness and are linked to sublimation defined as a direct vicissitude of the drive rather than as a defensive socially acceptable substitution. Wu or Mu as emptiness represents a marriage between sublimation and the Real, or the constructive or symbolic aspect of the death drive.

DOI: 10.4324/9781003198765-8

Lacan, in fact, directs us to the actual Vedanta or Hindu reference that predates the development of Nirvana and other more general Buddhist teachings he mobilizes in this lecture:

> If there is an object of thy desire, it's nothing but thine own self. This, however, is not the original characteristic of Buddhism. '*Tat Tvam Asi*' (You are That), the that which thou dost recognize in the other is thyself, is already set down in Vedanta.
>
> (idem)

The Vedanta or Hindu principle "You are That" is one of the references for Lacan's phrase "I am an Other" that he borrowed from Rimbaud, the French poet. The Other or "That" is where the ego is not, and where the subject is represented by the signifier. The Other of the signifier, as a shifter, could mean different things: a parent, the Unconscious, Society, or the Symbolic order, social or sexual difference, etc. When the signifier replaces and represents the subject, the subject of the Real fades before the signifier and becomes the subject of jouissance. Jouissance and the Real reveal something more than the reality ego; and the Other, in this case, is empty or inexistent, and exists only as a form of jouissance (Other jouissance). Fink observes this dynamic of the subject of the Real and Other jouissance in Lacan's Seminar on "The Purloined Letter," noting that:

> Lacan states that a signifier marks the cancellation of what it signifies; *ne* and "but" sign the death sentence of *the subject of the unconscious*. The latter subsists only long enough to protest, to say "No". Once the subject has said his or her piece, what he or she has said usurps his or her place; the signifier replaces him or her; he or she vanishes.
>
> (Fink, 1995, p. 41)

The subject is barred by language ($) and vanishes beneath or behind the signifier "no" or *ne* in French. The subject of the enunciation disagrees or denies the statement because the statement conflicts with other repressed signifiers or because the signifier fails to represent the subject of jouissance outside the signifier. The subject of the Real or the subject of jouissance "has no other being than as a breach in discourse," as Fink says (idem).

Like this "no," the "That" of Hinduism refers to the higher Self rather than the ego. The higher Self or the Unconscious mind points to the problems of the ego. However, Buddhism privileges not a higher Self but rather a big Mind (Chan and the Unconscious), which does not represent anything substantial that might refer to a self. If there is anything like a higher Self, it is an emptiness always under erasure by an assemblage of processes and experiences. No-self means no ego, and jouissance, or the subject in the Real, cannot be grasped as a form of self without significant inconvenience and shame to the subject. Therefore, the "This" in Buddhism must not be reduced to the idea of a higher Self. "This" in

Buddhism seen through psychoanalysis, or the Unconscious in psychoanalysis seen through Buddhism, departs from Jung's and Hinduism's references to "That" as a higher Self.

Dongshan's corresponding aphorism in Buddhism is "Just This." "Just This" is consistent with the Buddhist teaching of no-self and Lacan recognizes this when he comments, "This, however, is not the original characteristic of Buddhism" (in the reference to "You are That") (Lacan, 1962–1963, p. 223). By interjecting "I am not," Lacan is in fact giving us an original feature of Buddhism. The teaching of no-self means two different things within the Lacanian corpus. First, the subject is replaced by the signifier; and second, the subject of jouissance is outside discourse, or represents a discourse without words. "Just This" represents a non-dual experience between the signifier or form and the subject of jouissance or emptiness. By underlining what he is not-saying rather than what he is saying, he is in fact pointing to an original feature of Chan and the form of negation presented in the koan on Mu.

The critical saying "Just this" (就是这样, Jiùshì zhèyàng) is an answer that signifies the "mountain-still meditation state" that Dongshan promulgated during the Tang dynasty. The noble mountain (Dongshan) looks fixed without movement, yet the mountain is in flow, movement, or is jouissance. Despite the mountain being a Real obstacle (you have to go around or over it), the mountain is flowing not as an obstacle, but as a slender trace of jouissance that reveals that the river stands still, and the mountain is moving: Wu. This jouissance can be experienced in the ascent to the top of the mountain, and at the top of the mountain, however difficult the climb may have been. The mountain-still state is realized in the practice, rather than thinking about the mountain as a reality obstacle that cannot be broached.

In Lacanian terms, "Just This" refers not to the "true Self" but to a slender trace of jouissance that we all must take responsibility for. Responsibility for jouissance is taken through the function of Nomination as a form of metaphor without substitution. The subject of the Real as a body of jouissance is represented by the Name of the subject more than the signifier, and this is what seems disconcerting and abstract about the teaching of no-self. We can always come back to the Name that represents the body of the subject. However, the Name in the case of the knot of four is no longer a shifter like the signifier. Instead, it constitutes an S_1 with an anchor or tail in the body of jouissance constructed in lieu of another S_2 in the Symbolic. The signified is in the body rather than another signifier. The Name as a mental signifier is more body than cognition and provides a stable reference and orientation to the intensities associated with jouissance. The subject of jouissance outside the signifier is "This" or this traceless trace of jouissance. To call "This" no-self rather than a higher Self acts as a barrier to prevent the ego from appropriating emptiness, as hard to imagine as this may be. Emptiness is difficult to apprehend and appropriate as a concept, let alone as a form of self.

The experience of jouissance that Freud and Lacan had in front of an inanimate statue points to the jouissance-value of an experience of non-duality. Lacan writes, "This experience constituted around this statue, an experience I had myself, is characteristic and is usable by us" (2014, p. 227). The Moses of Michelangelo or the statue of a bodhisattva functions as a mirror that evokes a jouissance in the subject. On this point, Lacan recounts:

> I do not know if this statue I've given you in these photographs has succeeded in establishing for you this quivering, this communication that I assure you one can be quite sensitive to in its presence (Lacan, 1962–1963, p. 227); therefore, let us recover our serenity.
>
> (Lacan, trans. by Gallagher, 08.05.63 XVII 157)

Here we find, without searching, Lacan's mention of his own sensitivity and serenity as a subject.

Chapter 9

The Paradoxical Chan Koans, Self-Reference, and Letter Jouissance

Koan language often appears enigmatic or paradoxical. Perhaps it is this language feature that prompts North American cognitive scientist and literary scholar Douglas R. Hofstadter to present a discussion of Chan in his book, *Gödel, Escher, Bach: an Eternal Golden Braid* (GEB), which has little to do with Buddhism but is about how formal systems acquire meaning and, paralleling these processes, how consciousness emerges from meaningless symbols. While the discussion of Chan is not particularly extensive, it occupies a very special position. It appears first in the fictive dialogue between Achilles and the Tortoise at the end of Chapter VIII, the penultimate chapter of the first part titled "A Mu Offering." It then appears again in the main body of the following chapter, the last chapter of the first part titled "Mumon and Gödel." There, Hofstadter discusses the paradoxical language of Chan Buddhism to introduce Gödel-numbering, one of the fundamental ideas of the book.

While Hofstadter's aim is to introduce Gödel's theorem, his main concern is the generation of human consciousness, represented as the "I". He writes, "GEB is in essence a long proposal of strange loops as a metaphor for how selfhood originates" (Hofstadter, 1999, p. 7). What is most fascinating here is how Hofstadter uses the Gödelian idea to help us understand the phenomenon and the concept of the "I" through a discussion of paradox in language. We draw on this intersection to examine the paradoxical nature of language and the "I" as presented in Chan koans, and then compare how this paradox is presented in Hofstadter's book and in psychoanalysis.

At the end of Chapter VIII in GEB, Hofstadter creates a fictive dialogue between Achilles and the Tortoise to present the paradoxical feature of Chan koans. We know that the two distant names become a pair because of the well-known Zeno Paradox where the fleet-footed Achilles is never able to catch up with the Tortoise. It is a typical instance of the classical sophism that involves the infinite subdivision of distance. Here in Hofstadter's dialogue, Achilles appears in the robe of a Chan monk, and shares with his friend, two Chan koans.

The first, which we discussed previously, is the famous koan from the Chan master *Chao-chou* (Joshu). A monk asked him, "Does a dog have Buddha-nature or not?" The master answered, "Wu." This single word answer, "Wu," is often considered enigmatic because it seems to construct the answer as a paradox as

DOI: 10.4324/9781003198765-9

such: no answer or no asking is the answer. However, the Chan teacher does give the answer, even if it is not an ordinary one. "Wu" is an answer of the negative rather than a direct negation. Wu is not negating a concrete thing or perspective (a dog's capacity to "have"). Instead, it presents a perspective of the negative that breaks the dualism of having or not having. Obviously the slow, ignorant Tortoise could not jump beyond dualism and understand "Wu" as a unary negation upon first hearing.

The second koan recited by Hofstadter's Achilles has two versions. One is, "What is Buddha?" "This mind is Buddha" (即心即佛). The other is, "What is Buddha?" "This mind is no Buddha" (即心非佛). The two koans confuse the Tortoise even more because the meanings of the two answers directly oppose each other. The two versions of this koan, however, are another example for Hofstadter of how Chan goes beyond dualism. "This mind is Buddha" means do not seek Buddha outside because *prajna* only exists in self-nature. At the same time, this mind as self-nature is the pure mind of emptiness. This mind is Wu, and so it is also true to say, "This mind is no Buddha."

Although the two koans are different in content, they share a subtle insight about understanding. The answers, whether articulated with the single word "Wu" or by putting opposite answers together, break the linear logic that we expect to find from ordinary dialogues. The answers to these two koan questions seem to come from another realm of understanding that appears in the gap between the expected answer and the answer "as it is." This latter form of answer subtly and abruptly breaks the connection between the word and its meaning.

This break between the word and its meaning manifests a sharp distinction between the signifier and the signified. In his essay "The Instance of the Letter," Lacan makes this point very clear in the following sentence: "the S and s of the Saussurian algorithm are not in the same plane" (Lacan, 1966a, p. 430). This profound understanding of the absolute difference between the signifier and the signified is pivotal for psychoanalytic practice. It reveals the logic underlying the complicated metonymic displacement found in dreams and speech, and the inevitable division of the subject along the chains from S_1 to S_2.

While psychoanalysis exposes this break in a winding defensive process of free association, the language of Chan koan produced in the dialogue between teacher and student brings this collision of two signifiers directly in front of our eyes. This sudden collision of signifiers is a typical language style for both koans and its commentary poems. Indeed, Hofstadter notices that the commentary poems are as difficult as the koans. Chan refuses to compromise with language. If you want to "understand" a koan based upon meaning, you will most probably fail. The koan language is pure symbolic language in that image, expressions, and even actions are signifiers rather than signifieds.

Let us look at the following koan as another example:

Zen Master *Longtan* lit a candle for his student *Deshan*. Just as *Deshan* reached out to get it, the master blew out the candle. *Deshan* was suddenly enlightened. He knelt and bowed to his teacher. The master asked, "What did you see?" The student replied: "From now on, I will never doubt the tongues of all Chan masters in the world". The next day *Deshan* burned all the Chan notes he had. When the flames rose, he said: "All metaphorical arguments are only a fragment lost into the great void, and all world knowledge is a drop cast on a huge gully."

(Trans. from Xing Yun, p. 9)

Here, the action "light up the candle" means more than simply bringing light into darkness. Blowing out the candle as *Deshan* reaches for it nullifies both the candle's flame and the student's embrace and attachment to light and its differentiation from darkness. Striving for light, or enlightenment differentiated from darkness or ignorance, is contrary to Chan teachings, which regard the dark as absolute, and the light as relative. Light brings intellect but discriminates. Darkness is frightening but non-discriminating. Darkness gives wisdom without the ego. Thus, when asked by the teacher "What did you see?", the enlightened student did not answer it directly, or as we say, did not answer with the signified.

The movement from the signified to the signifier in the koan can be interpreted psychoanalytically at the point when "*Deshan* was suddenly enlightened." This enlightenment brings up a new signifying chain that leads *Deshan* into a wholehearted belief in Chan words, or what he describes as "the tongues of all Chan masters." At that moment of enlightenment, *Deshan*'s self was subsumed into the radiance of the Dharma teaching. Further, "the next day," *Deshan*'s belief leads him to another understanding of Chan, which compels him to "burn all the Chan notes he had." This seems to oppose his acknowledgment in the first part of the signifying chain of "the tongues of all Chan masters." However, this opposition or contradictory enlightened behavior appears as such insofar as "The next day" is heard as a signified. If we hear it instead as a signifier that does not refer to chronological time, but a logical moment of further enlightenment, then the opposition dissolves. For *Deshan*, from "today" to "the next day" is the time needed for a purely symbolic and purely Chan understanding to be articulated. He burned all his Chan notes because the Real jouissance of Chan goes beyond enlightenment in words and subjective experience. The Real happiness in Chan is the "great void and the huge gully" where there is no discrimination between light and dark, knowledge and world, word teaching and personal experience. There is only emptiness, only Wu.

The Tortoise in Hofstadter's fictive dialogue cannot grasp how the pure empty nature of Chan is articulated in the break between the signified and the symbolic koan words. Since the Tortoise is attracted to the logical dilemma presented in the koans, Achilles attempts to provide another approach. Achilles recounts how his master, *Okanisama*, also thought that only one of the two koans could be true. In addition, the master taught him how to judge the true answer. We can say that Achilles's master, the fictive seventh ancestor in Hofstadter's invention, is not a "genuine" Chan master if he takes only one as the genuine koan.

At the same time, proceduralizing resolution to koan paradoxes is how Hofstadter transitions from this koan-inspired dialogue between the Tortoise and Achilles into a discussion of Gödel's theorem of incompleteness and its applicability to language. According to Gödel's discovery, any word sequence, including one derived from the words of a koan, can be transcribed into a string of symbols, and therefore will comply with Gödel's theory of incompleteness as a result. As Hofstadter explains:

> Relying on words to lead you to the truth is like relying on an incomplete formal system to lead you to the truth. A formal system will give you some truth, but as we shall soon see, a formal system – no matter how powerful – cannot lead to all truth.
>
> (Hofstadter, 1979, p. 252)

This suggests that a formal system cannot lead to all truth inscribed in the koans. Similarly, koans, as texts composed of words, cannot reach all Chan Truth. Psychoanalytically speaking, the words in a koan can only reach what is representationally true but cannot reach the Truth of jouissance outside the signifier.

Here, Hofstadter's conclusion seems to provide support for the well-known Chan saying: "the text does not stand." And Hofstadter's exploration of Chan koans, supported by Gödel's groundbreaking theorem, seems to formalize this understanding in a rigorous mathematical proof of sorts.

Still, these points are rather ambiguous in GEB and have caused some amount of misunderstanding among his readers, some of whom have thought Hofstadter himself to be a monk. Hofstadter, subsequently, defended himself in the 20th-anniversary preface to GEB by declaring that he was not advocating for Chan. Despite Hofstadter's declaration, something remains from his analysis of the koan: the point that the truth is always half said. And with this observation, we return to the paradoxical nature of language itself as exposed by Chan koans, as well as the phenomenon of paradox in psychoanalysis and how this supplements our understanding of the koans.

According to Lacan, psychoanalysis uniquely contributes to the study of the paradoxical relationship between language and speech. In his essay "The Function and Field of Speech and Language in Psychoanalysis," known usually as the "Rome Report," Lacan lists three paradoxes between language and speech. The first paradox is the paradox of language and speech in psychosis. The psychotic patient seems to enjoy the absolute freedom of speech because his speech is beyond the limit of the symbolic Name of the Father. However, the absoluteness of this speech takes subjective delusions as its base. In this way, psychotic speech objectifies the subject into a kind of language that is devoid of a real logical structure or predicate logic. Therefore, although the psychotic keeps talking, his speech does not function.

In Lacan's words, the speech of psychosis is absent because the subject is spoken rather than speaks, and this has a negative effect on the subject's relationship to language. As a kind of delusional false speech, psychotic speech cannot produce effective free association because the symbolic function of discourse is blocked. In other words, the symbols used in psychotic language are not the signifiers of the unconscious, but the "signals" or noises of various delusive collisions. In a gesture of despair and hallucinatory thinking, the psychotic struggles to preserve his language from decaying. In this context, the analyst is responsible for seeing through the fraud covering over the foreclosure of the NoF.

We find a second paradox in psychoanalysis with the various representations of neurosis. The existence of repressed speech becomes manifest in the neurotic's speech. The speech of the neurotic is also the speech or discourse of the Other (the Unconscious) that for Lacan is also a "fully functioning speech" (*Ecrits*, 2006a, p. 232). Therefore, the neurotic's speech can and needs to be deciphered or interpreted. The deciphering and the interpretation of the speech bring about the unconscious structure of the subject and all the issues around desire.

And then, finally, the third paradox is the paradox of the subject in modern scientific discourse. Since Freud, psychoanalysis has been engaged in capturing truth with discourse and thereby establishing a new order for the sciences. We can even say that the paradox of the subject, to a certain extent, is also the paradox of the position of psychoanalysis in modern science because it is a paradox of the alienation of the subject under modern and scientific forms of objectification. According to Lacan, the subject's dilemma in modern scientific discourse is that the speaking subject is in danger of sliding from the position of the I (*Je*) to the *moi* (ego), that is, being "reduced to the words that signify it" (Lacan, 1966, p. 234). Truth claims regarding desire in this psychoanalytic context are necessarily incomplete. However, because the incompleteness and lack associated with desire cannot be objectively proven according to objectified measurable criteria, the truths of desire contained and revealed in analysis are not yet accepted as valid forms of scientific knowledge.

Lacan's discussions of these paradoxes are fundamentally related to language and speech. They are more concerned with the Symbolic in Lacan's conceptual framework of RSI. In Lacan's later thought, we find his concern shift from the Symbolic to the Real. In his seminar XXIII, Lacan asks, "Why then do I put this 'ex-sistence' precisely right where it might seem to be most paradoxical?" (Lacan, 2016, p. 38). He answers, "It is because I have to share out these three modes, and it is precisely on account of 'ex-sisting' that pondering the real is sustained" (idem). Lacan suggests that it is the Real that is the most paradoxical and the paradox of the Real lies in its "ex-sistence." In the RSI triad, the Real gives a new order to the Imaginary and the Symbolic, but the moment it is tied to them, they resist it. Therefore, the Real can only "ex-sist." It ex-sists in the way of encountering, of being the gap within the Symbolic rather than a Symbolic element. This also explains why when we ponder the Real, the Real escapes. It cannot be fully captured by the signifying chain. In Chan, the Real can only show up as a moment of enlightenment of mind or a bodily jouissance.

Lacan depicts the radical paradox of the Real as both coexisting and "existing" with two kinds of Borromean knots. In the three-component Borromean knot, the paradox is mainly around the Symbolic, as shown in the relationship between language and speech discussed earlier. The Symbolic gives the order, but at the same time it splits the subject. In this split it creates a hole in the knot, but it is a false one because what the hole marks is the subject, eternally falling off along the enclosed chain of signifiers.

In the four-component Borromean knot, the paradox is around the Real. This fourth element is the sinthome. When this element is knotted around the Symbolic, as shown by one of Lacan's planar diagrams in Seminar XXIII, it brings forth a new link and consistency. The sinthome is therefore not an additional element to the three, but the least requirement, in Lacan's words, "the minimum requirement" (idem), for a new three to be constituted. Lacan also stresses that the Real itself is meaningless. It is only a surface, a holding together. In this way, it stops the signifying chain from S_1 to S_2 and leads S_1 instead to S_0. S_0 here represents a jouissance outside the signifier that both reorganizes the internal relations of the signifier and represents the absence of meaning or the signified within the signifier.

Lacan's shift to the paradox of the Real from the paradox of the Symbolic allows psychoanalysis to use the Real's "ex-*sistence*" to open the enclosure of the Symbolic. Lacan's idea of the sinthome is critical to understand this shift. In Seminar XXIII, Lacan explains the paradoxical nature of the sinthome with the example of James Joyce, who "remains deeply rooted in his father while still disowning him" (idem, p. 55). Lacan reads Joyce to have, over the course of his life, foreclosed the meaning of the father and any order constructed by the Symbolic. Joyce expresses this in a letter to his wife, Nora: "My mind rejects the whole present social order and Christianity's home, the recognized virtues, classes of life, and religious doctrines" (Maddox, 1988, p. 1). This foreclosing gesture may indicate a psychotic structure characterized by a mind that has completely discarded the Symbolic Name of the Father.

But reading Joyce to represent the paradox of psychosis in relationship to the Symbolic does not completely explain Joyce's speech. His writing is clearly not delusional speech. Although it is written in a language that seems always ready to disintegrate itself, it nonetheless possesses the very texture of literariness. Joyce's speech bears something unique about a subject that goes beyond the Symbolic. In Lacan's opinion, Joyce "canceled his subscription to the unconscious" (Lacan, 2018, p. 144), or what we can also refer to as the repressed Freudian unconscious. For Lacan, Joyce is thus "an *a*-Freud."

This cancellation is not embodied by an aggressive social gesture. Instead, it is embodied in a radical act of writing. It demonstrates that the unconscious level of language exists in phonation, while the writing effectuates a perennial stopping of the phonatory identification with language. Joyce, for example, makes up a word composed of 100 letters to demonstrate his horror of lightning; or, in his impossible novel, *Finnegans Wake*, Joyce mobilizes 60 different languages to create new terms and expressions. Joyce is doing the impossible work of castrating language from the very place where the subject is produced.

While Joyce is "an *a*-Freud," Joyce is not an *a*-Lacan. Lacan seldom identified himself with anyone throughout his career or in his seminars. But in his lecture "Joyce the Symptom" delivered in 1975, we find a different Lacan, a Lacan who, despite himself, touchingly related to Joyce in a personal way. He concluded, "Pardon me for telling my tale, but I think I'm doing it only in homage to James Joyce" (p. 142), after discussing how he believed the religious background he and Joyce shared shaped their common destiny (idem).

Elsewhere in the lecture, Lacan explained that he and Joyce were involved in the same activity when they created and played with word riddles. "He put it there because, just after, there's another word. In short, it's exactly like my business of *osbject, mendation, dit-mention,* and all the rest" (idem, p. 132). Lacan even admitted that he was able to touch on something he hadn't thought of before because of Joyce (idem). This something is the sinthome. In fact, Lacan goes so far as to suggest that Joyce is the symptom, emphasizing the homophonic relation between "*ptom*" and the French word *p'tithomme* (idem, p. 141), meaning "small person." This "small person" or "*ptom*" is the ego in Lacan's psychoanalytic category and exists universally in everyone. But with his unique writings, Joyce succeeds in transforming his ego-symptom into a sinthome, which homophonically carries the meaning "a saintly person," which Lacan theorizes as a subject of the Real.

Joyce's writing is exceptional for Lacan because it establishes an eternal literary name by disrupting language in its very structure. In Joyce's hands, sentences are smashed into words and words into letters. From there, the very place of letter jouissance emerges and flows back into the Symbolic. Lacan says, "Read a few pages of *Finnegans Wake* without striving to understand it. It is quite readable, as someone from my circle remarked to me, because one can sense the presence of the jouissance of the he that wrote it" (idem, p. 144). As Lacan indicates, Joyce's writing substantializes a new way of understanding. It is not an understanding "hooking anything of your unconscious" (idem, p. 145) but a pure enjoyment of the words or sounds themselves.

In this sense, the letter becomes what Lacan calls the litter. The litter is the thing that has no service for the repressed unconscious. For Joyce, the Name of the Father is foreclosed from the Symbolic, but his writing is open to the Name of the Father coming from the Real. This NoF in the Real revives the Symbolic NoF and therefore becomes the father of the name. What Joyce fulfills is not the fate of the subject but the destiny of the "I" in the Real. This "I," Lacan calls it, the Ego, or alternatively we call it a subject of the Real. It is through this Ego that James realizes himself. This is the exact meaning of self-reference in psychoanalysis. Self-reference here means going from the imaginary ego to the subject of the signifier, and from the subject of the signifier to the subject of jouissance.

It is with this special "I," this big Mind, that we can now return to Hofstadter. As we mentioned, what underlies Hofstadter's exploration of the paradox of Chan koans is Gödel's theorem that the true goes beyond language as a formal system. Formal system here does not mean a complete and formal logical system (i.e., Hilbert's logical project that Gödel critiqued), but a system composed of symbols without meaning and certain artificial rules that bind these symbols together. The function of a formal system as such lies in the fact that it can avoid the ambiguity caused by natural language.

With Frege's accurate logical articulation of quantifiers with symbols, and Cantor's theory of set and understanding of the different layers of infinity, Gödel successfully transcribed all mathematical propositions in Russell and Whitehead's PM into numbers. In this way, Gödel realizes the impossible task of talking about mathematics with mathematics. This is what we can understand as Gödelian self-reference. Here, self-reference refers to Real mathematical symbols outside language, but not to a jouissance simultaneously accessible both through and outside language or symbols. Lacanian self-referentiality embodied by Joyce's writing is in the form of a jouissance, which is at once accessed through letters and substantializes the subject of the Real beyond letters. The Real escapes the self-reference provided by letters and yet can also be revealed by letters.

Modern mathematicians and logicians such as Bertrand Russell and Alfred Tarski identified self-reference as the cause of paradox and attempted to transcend it. The aim of Gödel's work was different. In his transcription of mathematical propositions into integers, self-reference was produced rather than avoided. Gödel found that there are at most three layers of meaning in a mathematical proposition and that all three layers could be expressed in integers in his numbering system. Therefore, every mathematical proposition corresponds to a single Gödelian number. At the same time, the Gödelian number itself is an integer, no matter how big it is. In this way, self-reference is realized as a paradox but through a different system of meaning.

Hofstadter is taken by Gödel's realization of self-reference with and in numbers. He tries to determine patterns from Gödel's proof process and finds what he calls "tangled hierarchies." Hofstadter describes them as "strange loops." He observes that we can move along the hierarches of the loop ad infinitum, but unexpectedly, we also find ourselves right back at the starting point. Of these strange loops, he notes, "there is a conflict between the finite and the infinite, and hence a strong sense of paradox" (Hofstadter, 1999, p. 15). Paradox is caused by the failure of the human cognitive structure (*connaissance*) or consciousness to trace the finite all the way to infinity, on the one hand. On the other hand, the same consciousness can abstractly realize the infinite within the finite, or the emptiness within form. While paradox is a blocked sense forced upon by the Symbolic, in the Real, a paradox is no longer because *connaissance* is replaced with *savior*.

Hofstadter's "tangled hierarchies" share certain qualities with Lacan's three registers represented by Borromean Loops. Hierarchy here does not conform to an intuitive understanding of moving from simple to complex. Rather, it signifies absolute difference between different levels woven together. Lacan's loops also display this feature of hierarchy. When talking about the knot as the support of the subject, Lacan says:

> What is marked out by color is not the difference of each one from the next, but rather their absolute difference, as it were, in so far as it is a difference common to all three of them. It is only when something is introduced to mark out the difference between the three of them, as opposed to difference at the level of the twain, that there appears as a consequence of the distinction between two structures of the Borromean knot.
>
> (Lacan, 2018, p. 40)

The three registers, the Real, the Symbolic and the Imaginary, are sharply different. But with the dominance of the Symbolic, in the narrative lower chain of signifiers in the graph of desire, this difference is erased into a smooth topological surface. Imaginary fantasies, following the displacement of signifiers, function also to provide a consistency for the three. But this is a false consistency. In the clinical work of psychoanalysis, a Real cut is thus introduced to break this false consistency.

Lacan's second Borromean structure adds to the first an exception that Gödel's embrace of self-referentiality helps us to understand. The Gödelian translation of numbers back to propositions demonstrates that although different hierarchies of meaning can be articulated in numbers, this equivalence comes from an exception at the very beginning. This exception is given in the original proposition "that I cannot be proved." I am true because I cannot be proven, or in Chan language, true self is no-self. All formal processes start from this sheer, unconditional negative.

This is also what Lacan says about the Name of the Father from the Real. In the new Borromean knot, the father is the sinthome, emerging from a sheer negative, that "ex-sists" as a structuring hole within the Symbolic. Thus, the subject of the sinthome is the non-supposed subject, what Lacan calls the real Ego or the subject of and in the Real. The subject is always supported by the imaginary ego and the subject of the signifier, but the fourth term of the sinthome marks the real Ego or the subject of the Real.

Before continuing, we would like to further clarify how Lacan uses the Freudian concept of the ego in Seminar XXIII. Up until that seminar, we had been used to Lacan's significant elaborations of the Freudian concepts of the ideal ego and ego ideal by way of "mathemes." He shifts from this focus with the definition of this new Real ego produced from analyzing Joyce's writing. In fact, Lacan starts his seminar by noting that the synthetic function of the ego ordinarily found in everyday uses of language, or what Freud refers to as the reality ego, is missing in Joyce and in psychoses, and this is what makes his writing incomprehensible or unreadable. Instead, Lacan reads the Ego in Joyce's writing to be functioning at a different level as an enigma or as what creates riddles.

While formal writing is typically approached as a reflection of the synthetic function of the ego and the acceptance of established uses of writing, for Joyce, it is the writing itself that performs an enigmatic function. Writing in Joyce stands in lieu of the unified image of the body that has the double distinction of representing an early form of narcissism and a synthesis between fantasy and reality. While the Freudian ego is narcissistic because the body has been captured as an image that performs a fantasy function and yet anchors the subject in social reality, in the Real ego Lacan observes in Joyce the synthesis between fantasy and social reality takes place at the level of his writing and not of his ego or body image in the ordinary sense.

Lacan goes on in Seminar XXIII to say that the definition of the signifier as what represents a subject to another signifier is implicated in the division of the subject. When the signifier represents the subject, the subject of jouissance vanishes other than as a signifier. Joyce's writing reveals how the signifier can perform a linking or synthetic function at a symbolic and mental rather than imaginary bodily dimension. In Freud, this symbolic dimension of the subject within language is understood as a form of reality ego and where the linking function is attributed to the ego rather than to the symbolic function. Lacan takes this a step further by attributing the synthetic linking function to the Real of jouissance that we mistake for an ordinary ego. The subject's experience of the Real lies both outside the image of the ego, and outside the signifier that fails to represent the subject of jouissance outside the signifier. In this sense, the enigmatic linking function of the new Real ego refers to the linking function of Lacan's second definition of the Real and of an Other jouissance as a form of the Life drive. We use the term "subject of the Real" to distinguish between the Freudian concept of the ego and Lacan's new Real ego.

With this clarity, we can now return to discussing Joyce as a representative of the sinthome. Joyce realizes a new style of writing by smashing words into letters, and then letting letters get together in a free associative way to block ordinary understanding, or to go beyond our ordinary egoic expectation of words. This produces a text free from the metonymic weaving of unconscious desire. The text, instead, is organized by jouissance contained within letters.

Letters, like particles, emerge from points of increased density within fields of jouissance that remain outside letters, while being "affected" by them at the same time. Electron flow, for example, takes place from atom to atom as each atom receives and spits out or sprays a new electron, and generating what is known as an electrical current. An electrical current can produce a magnetic field, and, in turn, a magnetic field can generate an electrical current as well. Similarly, a flow of signification can produce a field of jouissance, and a field of jouissance can generate a flow of signification.

Letters represent chains of inanimate matter (marks in the sand, ink on paper) insofar as organized letters and marks have lost and replaced a direct and immediate connection to the world. Hofstadter is concerned with how the animate or life emerges out of inanimate letters, and Lacan is concerned with how the subject is constituted by symbolic letters representing the death drive.

Letters are the fundamental unit in writing by which the object world is entirely replaced by signifiers. Letters can be considered the beginning of culture, predicate language, and human cognition or consciousness. However, just like initial speech sounds or phonemes are organized into a system of sounds, and sounds are organized into an alphabet, so are letters organized into a system or battery of signifiers, words, and signifying differentiations, all of which are constitutive of the experiences of a subject.

Chapter 10

The True Body of Bodhi and Buddh(*a*)

Both the Chan teaching of Mu and *Dongshan*'s "Just This" require a certain knowledge and knowing in and with the body. The physiological or physical experience of the body cannot be separated from an act of understanding. Indeed, in Sanskrit, the root "*budh*" denotes both to wake up and to know, and bodhi means enlightenment, which is also a form of insight or cognition embedded in the body. Buddha means awakening to enlightenment in and with the body. However, to say enlightenment with the body is also not correct, since enlightenment is also realized with the mind, and not just the body. In this sense, emphasizing mind or body are both wrong. Thus, the better description of enlightenment is Dogen's body and mind dropped off.

For Dogen, the true human body comes from an act of understanding through which body and mind are dropped off or fall off. Dogen refers to this as a naked bodily experience. Lacan refers to how Joyce's body and mind are shed when he is subjected to a beating. In addition, in these examples, the signifier is incorporated into what Lacan calls the body of thought. The incorporeal signifier shapes the enlightened body into accord with the body of the signifier. The true human body comes forth from this specific act of understanding (emptiness). In emptiness, the true human body (not to be mistaken with crude biological instincts or physiological drives) functions freely and automatically in accord with the entire universe.

Chan teachers should be constantly hinting at what cannot be said, rather than simply passing over it in silence, as Wittgenstein recommended. Philosophic and religious enterprises consist in fidelity to the inexpressible and to the search for "expressibility" in language. Strictly speaking, this is an impossible task, "yet it had been carried out, because it was a mode of compassion that Dogen so eloquently expounded as 'loving speech' (*aigo*)" (Kim, 2004, p. 95). Buddhas expound the unsayable in a saying out of loving kindness for all beings. Speaking beings, however, tend to reject what they do not understand, leading to a rejection of Buddha's paradoxical non-dual teaching. Thus, the intellect needs to be purified to accept and use what cannot be formulated in words other than as a form of negation or "nay-saying."

In Chan, the purification of mind and speech is achieved and reinforced by the experience of meditation or just sitting. Dogen described the non-duality between

DOI: 10.4324/9781003198765-10

speech and the state beyond words in his 1237 essay "*Tenzo Kyokun*" (Instructions for the Cook):

> The monastics of future generations will be able to understand a non-discriminative Zen (*ichimizen*) based on words and letters, if they devote efforts to spiritual practice by seeing the universe through words and letters and words and letters through the universe.
>
> (p. 100)

Because of the intrinsic duality of language, speech often leads to misunderstandings and miscommunication between people. However, to say that Chan abides by the opposite hypothesis of silence or non-assertion would not be correct either. This is the import of Dogen's non-discriminative use of words and language. The challenge for Chan is how to use words in a non-discriminative way that promotes a feeling of agreement or accord even when individuals may have different forms of understanding.

In a system in which non-assertion is one of the marks of enlightenment, one must always remember that non-assertion is not put forward as a positive theory or as a metaphysical system. This sublime doctrine is not a cockpit for logicians, who supposedly use the doctrine of emptiness not to support one theory against others, but rather to discard them altogether. This is not the case in psychoanalysis. Psychoanalysis does not aspire to be atheoretical. The question remains as to whether this is true of Buddhism or Chan as well. Obviously, the Middle Way (Madhyamika philosophy) and Yogacara teachings are not atheoretical or anti-theoretical, even though the *Linji* Chan lineage likes to interpret Nagarjuna as proposing the destruction of all theory and logic. Moncayo (2012) has argued that the tetralemma does not propose the destruction of logic but the articulation of different dimensions and levels of logic and reason (idem).

For if Nirvana is not distinct from birth and death and is not a separate reality at all, then emptiness is neither the non-difference between 'yes' and 'no,' nor a truth that escapes us whether we affirm or deny it. Moreover, truth does not necessarily lie somewhere between affirmation and denial (although this may be the case in true forms of silence), and the person who dwells in emptiness does not always stay neutral with regard to affirming or denying something. A person who dwells in emptiness is not perturbed by others' opinions, while at the same time knows that non-duality must be revealed within negation, affirmation, and the dualities of language.

So long as the mind oscillates between contradictory statements, trying to determine which of them is true and which is false, the aspirant remains confined within the mundane. Instead, the subject must choose one of the sides of the contradictory statement or situation to reveal non-duality within the relative side of ordinary life. Through the practice of meditation, the intellect is bypassed and disappears from the mundane phenomenal plane and reappears in the transcendental yet ordinary domain of the emptiness of form.

Case 21 of the Book of Serenity is called "*Yunyan* Sweeps the Ground." The first part of the name *Yunyan* (Chinese: 云岩昙晟; pinyin: Yún yán tán sheng) comes from *Yunyan* Mountain, located outside modern-day Xian, which is what remains of the old city of *Changsha*. When *Yunyan* was sweeping the ground, *Daowu* (道无69–835 CE) said, "Too busy." *Yunyan* said, "You should know there's one who isn't busy." *Daowu* said, "If so, then there's a second moon." *Yunyan* held up the broom and said, "Which moon is this?"

"Too busy" here represents the phenomenal plane of assertion and trying to get things done, but the "too" in "too busy" suggests a form of assertion with some idea of attaining purity in the activity. The one who is not busy does not refer to another idle person, but to another *Yunyan* within *Yunyan* who is not busy because he stays calm during the sweeping activity. The one who is not busy is the emptiness within the phenomenal form of sweeping the ground.

Dogen's understanding of the body as an act of understanding is his way of expressing non-dual understanding within ordinary material forms recognizable to everyone. The very concept and word "body" represents an act of understanding. Focusing on the body also reveals Dogen's "Inter-sectarian" approach to Buddhism. The body is something shared by everyone regardless of denomination. "Zazen only" or *zuo Chan* is a primordial form of Buddha Dharma bound to no school. Zazen, as the supreme vehicle, can generally be understood as the fundamental source of insight, mindfulness, true compassion, and enlightenment leading to the act of understanding "body and mind dropped off." Finally, zazen, *zuo Chan*, or just sitting differs from how meditation appears in general Buddhism as one of the aspects of the threefold way of morality, meditation, and wisdom or meditation as one of the six perfections.

Reading another koan is instructive here. Chan master *Mayu Baoche* was using a fan. A monk asked, "The nature of the wind is eternal and there is no place where it doesn't reach. So why does the master use a fan?" Remember that Western science told us we live in the bottom of an ocean of air. *Baoche* said, "You know that the nature of wind is eternal, but you don't know that there's no place it doesn't reach." The monk said, "What is the principle of 'there is no place it doesn't reach'?" *Baoche* just fanned himself. The monk bowed and said, "Useless teachers and monks! There are a thousand of them. What are they good for?"

This koan teaches us how the wind or spirit of Buddhism is actualized in the small, everyday actions that manifest the ultimate reality of the universe. By fanning himself, the teacher is actualizing the golden nature of wind, without explaining it. The nature of wind is such that it cannot be conceptualized or contemplated but is instead to be actualized. Furthermore, it is not potentiality being actualized, but rather actuality creating itself through the act of fanning.

According to Dogen, Dharma did not and should not avoid intellectual let alone religious and existential involvement in conflicts concerning various interpretations and views. The non-committal way of life in this case would respect and avoid conflicts and blame them on Buddhism, whether rightly or wrongly, rather than bringing forth enlightenment out of the ground of personal conflicts and delusions. Personal questions about Dharma are never only pure and always carry along impure residues of the person's own obstacles and problems. Thus, Dogen wrote, "by and large, many sages are commonly concerned with the study of cutting off the root of entwined vines, but do not realize that cutting consists in cutting entwined vines with entwined vines." What obfuscates the truth of Dharma is not only poor expression or cognitive entanglements, but also a person's personal problems and attachments. The search for enlightenment is unavoidably mixed up with elements of delusion. We must understand entwining and twine vines with entwined vines and inherit Dharma in and through twine vines. The inheritance of Dharma resides precisely in entwined vines.

Chapter 11

The Mirror in Lacan, Chan, and Dogen's Zen

In his Seminar on Anxiety, Lacan (1962–1963) examines the function of the mirror shared by Chan and psychoanalysis. "Buddhist experience presupposes an eminent reference to the function of the mirror in our relationship to the object. Indeed, the metaphor is commonly employed therein" (p. 223). The mirror in Lacan's work on the mirror phase refers to a human-cast mirror, the specular body image represents the ideal ego, while the empty mirror itself (rather than the image) represents the empty Real that structures the relations between the image and the Name of the Other. Only the emptiness of the human-cast mirror in Lacan is linked to the Chan Mirror of mind. In Lacanian terms, the emptiness of the Real articulates a knot composed of the emptiness of the cast mirror, the body image, and the Name given to the subject.

In addition to the emptiness of the cast mirror and the specular image, Lacan (idem) also alludes to a surfaceless mirror in nature in which everything is reflected as a fabrication or artifice of the human Mind. "We know how easy it is for outside things to take on the complexion of our soul, and even its form, and even for them to come towards us in the shape of a double" (p. 223). We project human things to nature in animism through the surfaceless mirror that nature is. Animist traditions, for example, perceive the human spirit in, and attribute human agency to, water, rocks, trees, and fire. The surfaceless mirror in nature reflects us, and the clear mirror of Mind, or the Real emptiness of mind, reflects nature. The mirror in nature is surfaceless because it does not have the polished surface of a clear cast mirror. Nature and the earth can function as a mirror despite not having a uniform smooth surface.

Lacan's reference to a mirror in relationship to Buddhist experience, initially then, involves at least two types of mirrors, both of which are distinguishable from Chan's clear mirror Mind. The first is a clear cast mirror, made by humans, but also found in nature in the form of, for example, the cephalic eye as a mirror or reflective surface. And the second is the surfaceless mirror in Nature, which can be thought of as one made with water, rocks, metals, and eyes. This mirror points to nature itself, or the earth itself, being a giant mirror made of clouds and small pieces of rock and not only to the mirror of nature as solely a site for human projections.

DOI: 10.4324/9781003198765-11

The two types of mirrors are related, but different. As Lacan discusses, cephalic eyes, as a natural example of a cast mirror, began as a small opaque stain within mollusks and seashells:

> The appearance of the visual apparatus itself, at the level of the fringes of the lamellibranchiate (shell of an oyster), begins with a pigmentary stain, the first appearance of a differentiated organ in the sense of a sensibility which is already properly speaking visual. And, of course, there is nothing more blind than a stain!
>
> (Lacan, 1960–1961, p. 254)

While shells do not have cephalic or vertebrate eyes, they do have eyes of a simple structure, and the first appearance of such a visual apparatus manifests along the mantle fringes of the lamellibranchiate. Beyond the mirror in and of nature, cephalic vertebrate eyes began as a blind stain or sensitivity within shells. A blind stain, as the root of a cephalic eye, is a good metaphor or point of condensation for the blind surfaceless mirror in nature. The eye is already a mirror that evolved from the surfaceless mirror of nature.

The distinctions among the clear looking glass mirror or human-cast mirror, the eye of the specular image, and the surfaceless mirror in Nature we find in Lacan begs the question of how to think of them in relationship to the Ancient Mirror and Clear Mirror of Chan and Zen. We provide an extensive exploration of an answer to this question in this chapter.

We begin then by turning to fascicle 19 (*Kokyo* or "On the Ancient Mirror") of the *Shobogenzo* (*The Eye and Treasury of the True Law*). The *Shobogenzo* was unknown to the public and was kept by Dogen's family lineage for 400 years until first published in 1766. Zen teacher Dogen (1223–1227), who was the greatest 12th-century Japanese Soto Zen teacher and thinker, distinguished between two mirrors: the Ancient Mirror and the Clear Mirror. Although there are not two Mirrors, "the Ancient Mirror" refers to the Ancient Mirror, and "the Clear Mirror" refers to the Clear Mirror, a principle otherwise known as "Not one, not two."

Lacan's mirror of Nature *without* human projections can be understood as a form of the Ancient Mirror found in Chan. Put another way, Lacan's mirror of nature without projections is akin to the Ancient Mirror of Chan only when Nature is perceived by an unsubstantial and inexistent human Mind, and not by a human-made clear surface mirror like that of the mirror stage and the imaginary ego. In front of Lacan's clear human-cast mirror, the ideal ego seeks recognition from the Other's desire; while in front of the Ancient Mirror of Nature, or Lacan's mirror of Nature free of human projections, the Chan Mind and no-self can be realized.

The Chan clear mirror of Mind (not a cast mirror) represents the universe as the Ancient ancestral mirror, or the mirror of Nature that is not a human-cast mirror with projections. The human Chan Mind, where the mirror of Nature becomes the Ancient ancestral Mirror, is an insubstantial empty mirror. In contrast, for Lacan, the clear mirror is a material, human-cast empty reflective surface, where emptiness is defined as a surface without reflections. However, behind the eye as an organ or mirror-like surface lies not consciousness but what Chan calls Mind. The Chan Mind, like Lacan's Real, "ex-sists" outside symbolization and therefore can be described as inexistent in the Symbolic order. The clear mirror of the empty Mind does not retain symbolic or linguistic inscriptions registered in the back systems of the Mind (the Ucs. and Pcs., according to Freud).

The aspect of Mind that is neither a thing nor an apparatus, neither man-made nor reflection, "makes" the person. Dogen discusses how the human is born with a mirror on his or her back, where the mind as mirror is not a man-made self or reflection. Because the mirror is on the person's back, it is beyond human capacity to fabricate Chan Mind (or the second face of the Ancient Mirror), just as it is beyond human capacity to fabricate a universe (or the first face of the Ancient Mirror). Working through how the Clear Mirror and the Ancient Mirror appear and are handled in a classical Chan story helps us to better understand this aspect of Mind recognized by Lacan as that which is "habitual in Buddhism":

> Great Master *Seppō Shinkaku* once told his assembly, "If you want to understand this matter, our here-and-now existence is just like one face of the Ancient Mirror. When a foreigner comes, a foreigner appears in It; when a Han comes, a Han appears in It." *Gensha Shibi* then came forth and asked, "How about when you suddenly encounter a Clear Mirror coming towards you?" The Master replied, "Both foreigner and Han disappear." *Shibi* commented, "It is not that way with this one." *Seppō* asked, "How is it with you?" *Shibi* replied, "Please put my question to me, Reverend Monk." *Seppō* said, "How about when you suddenly encounter a Clear Mirror coming towards you?" *Shibi* answered, "It is shattered into hundreds of pieces!"
>
> (Dogen, 1241 [1998], p. 218)

The "hundreds of pieces" of the clear mirror Mind can be understood as the signifiers or Names that articulate the relationship between the body image and the emptiness of the mirror. The unity of the specular image must be transformed into a symbolic body of signifying units: from the completed unity to the unit of signification. The pieces also refer to how the forms of nature enlighten and reflect the nature of the symbolic subject, or the treasury of the signifier, rather than the imaginary ego. Again, the imaginary ego projects its representations unto the forms of nature, while the scientific and spiritual study of the forms of nature, incorporated into a body of signifiers and numbers, gives an accurate, objective, and subjective, symbolic account of the forms of nature.

In this sense, then, Dogen's story reveals not only a narrative, but the "place" or state of mind of a Real subject, at the subjective place of jouissance. The Ancient clear Mirror of Mind is the place of the Third jouissance. The Ancient clear Mirror of the human Chan Mind is the "What" that "parent and child," "teacher and student," and "analyst and analysand" are mastering together. The question can be reframed in this form: "What does a subject do when their Mind has become One bright clear mirror, or 'What' does a subject do when they encounter someone who is a bright clear mirror?" *Shibi* answered, "It is shattered into hundreds of pieces!" The saying "Break it into a thousand pieces," captures *Léthes* or the forgetting aspect of truth (*Aletheia*). Subjects forget about the mirror that remains in the background (as it were, on their backs), and simply live the details of their ordinary lives understanding the past in the present, and with an eye toward the future.

The oneness of the clear mirror is not "our" Mind in the sense of a mental ego, but Mind and mirror included in things. The clear mirror of Mind is reflected in the broken mirror embedded in many things, and the broken mirror that many things are, in turn, reflects the clear mirror of Mind. Dogen instructs:

> Let's begin by looking at and investigating *Seppō's* "Ancient Mirror". In his saying that our here-and-now existence is just like one face of the Ancient Mirror, "one face" means that boundaries have long been eliminated and that "within and without" have also been passed beyond; it is our being as a pearl rolling about on a flat board.
>
> (idem, p. 215)

> The Ancient Mirror does not depend on the comings and appearances of foreigners or Han, for "It" is every single thing's being as unobstructed as a bell's clear resounding in all directions. It is beyond being many, beyond being large.
>
> (idem, p. 224)

From one vantage, the Ancient Mirror can be grasped according to Dogen in *Seppō*'s saying that "our here-and-now existence is just like one face of the Ancient Mirror." Here-and-now existence *refers* to the Chan Mind interacting with the environment that represents the universe or the Ancestral mirror for a subject. The "one face" of this Ancestral mirror is "One" insofar as boundaries have long been eliminated and the "within and without" have also been passed beyond. Oneness in the Real is "our being as a pearl rolling about on a flat board" (idem, p. 215).

The Ancient Mirror can also be likened to the Mobius strip Lacan frequently references, as a surface that only has one side although it circulates between and within two. A Chan definition of the Mobius strip would be "Not one, not two." Our earlier reference to Dogen's idea that the Ancient mirror and the Chan mirror Mind are "not one, not two" can now be better understood as a topological principle. It is not one because the Mobius strip has an exterior and interior side, but it is not-two because it, nontheless, has only one side. Both Chan and psychoanalysis function within this topological structure. And an analyst must work within a topological structure that both has and has no boundaries between inside and outside, subject and Other. Topological boundaries differentiate analyst from analysand, and at the same time subject and Other are structurally interdependent and go into each Other. Both dimensions are required for analysis to bear therapeutic "truth-effects."

In Chan, the Universe is the first face of the Ancient Mirror, while this is not true for Lacanian psychoanalysis since Lacan said that psychoanalysis is not a cosmology or is "*a*cosmic," or more of a comic than an astronaut, however much humanity may need both. In Chan, a topological structure circulates between the Universe and the Ancestral Clear Mirror of Mind: the Universe is Mind and Mind is the Universe. In psychoanalysis, the subject or the signifier shifts in a flow of signification that carries the *objet a* that mediates the relationship to the object world. The *objet a* appears here "*qua latouse*" as a common object in the narrative, and over there, or in the "Other scene," as an unconscious object cause of desire that the Other is lacking.

The absence of an Imaginary dimension in Chan paradoxically leads to a paucity or brevity of the use of words in ordinary speech and the privileging of the sounds of silence. The fantasy or the Imaginary is not spoken about other than in symbolic terms. Psychoanalysis suffers from a not enough of the second Lacanian Real, while Chan suffers from an absence of fantasy and sexuality discussed either in intellectual terms, or in the terms used in ordinary speech. Fantasy in Chan is quickly sublimated into forms of the creative imagination. The downside of excluding fantasy from ordinary speech because of a fear of immoral speech is that it possibly leads to acting out the fantasy even as those fantasies have been concealed from speech because of the very same fear.

In addition to the one face of the mirror, and from another vantage point, Dogen also discusses a second clear face of the Ancient Mirror:

> The Ancient Mirror does not depend on the comings and appearances of foreigners or Han, for "It" is every single thing's being as unobstructed as a bell's clear resounding in all directions. It is beyond being many, beyond being large.
>
> (idem, p. 224)

If from the first vantage, the oneness of the Ancient Mirror is found in the smallness of a single pearl, here Dogen discusses it from the perspective of an uncountable vastness. The Ancestral clear mirror is not obstructed by distinctions between small or large, foreigner and Han, or for that matter, between ordinary people and sages, or even dragons and snakes. In Chan, dragons represent Buddhas while snakes represent ordinary people. At the same time, insofar as the snake (Naga) in Nagarjuna's teaching of non-duality represents the non-dual wisdom of emptiness, ordinary people become the place of a second clear face of the Ancient Mirror.

The Ancient Mirror in things is an eternal echo of being that appears in here-and-now experience. Having no boundary, it is beyond inside and outside. The Ancient Mirror resounds clearly in all directions as the unobstructed being of things. Buddha's daily activities take place within the Ancient Mirror. Any pebble, tile, metal, piece of wood, glass, or water, etc., interacts with human activity in such a way that the Ancient Mirror in them is polished into a clear mirror that is both subject and object at once. When the mirror in nature is polished into a clear mirror, then the outside becomes the inside, and the inside can be seen on the outside.

So essential is the mirror to articulating the Mind in Buddhism that Dogen discusses the physical possibility of its making, and the making of humans into Buddha, as the same. Here human technology and human evolution appear to manifest from similar principles.

> The virtue of making a Mirror was made manifest, for it was the diligent effort of an Ancestor of the Buddha. If polishing a tile did not make a Mirror, then even polishing a mirror could not have made a Mirror.

> (idem, p. 228)

> If a tile could not become a Mirror, people could not become Buddha. If we belittle tiles as being lumps of clay, we will also belittle people as being lumps of clay. If people have a Heart, then tiles too will have a Heart.

> (idem, p. 229)

Does a tile have an animate heart that reflects an intimate subjective experience, or is this how a tile is "animated" with human characteristics? To understand how fundamentally linked the physical qualities of the mirror are to the experiential qualities of human existence in this story, we propose that topology is a way of existence.

The flat or curved board, on which we are a pearl rolling about on a flow of signification, according to this Chan story, is also a metaphor for the Lacanian subject as a topological cross cap within which the *objet a* circulates. The subject is both the structure (of the dream) and one of its elements represented either by the cross cap or the *objet a*. The *objet a* (a part object representing the Other) circulates between inside and outside as the structure of the subject opens and closes. In this sense, both inside and outside are already included within the subject writ large (I am another). The subject writ large includes the *Umwelt* or the subjectively perceived environment.

The clear Mirror of Mind, or pearl, can be understood further in relationship to Lacan's "agalma," or as an aspect of the *objet a* in the Real. "The agalma is the object towards which the subject believes their desire aims and that carries to an extreme the misrecognition of the object cause of desire" (Lacan, 2005, p. 82). The agalma captures how the subject believes he or she sees his or her specular image, or the object cause of desire reflected in the mirror of the Other. Instead, we propose that the subject is searching for the emptiness of or in the Other (there where you believe I am an imaginary *objet a*, I am nothing).

In his Seminar VIII on Transference, Lacan (1960–1961) observes in Plato's *Symposium* that Alcibiades misrecognizes the object that Socrates represents for him. Where Alcibiades believes that Socrates has the imaginary object of his

desire, Socrates is simply "no-thing" or an empty clear mirror. Socrates's emptiness, or the *objet a* in the Real, can be recognized as an imaginary phallic object,
as well as an enlightened state of mind, a form of bliss or delight equivalent by
metaphor to an agalma, a translucid diamond or jewel. The phallus is the name of
the formless, and the signifier of a lack or emptiness. At the same time, the formless emptiness is the name for the symbolic phallus, as the function that represents
and sublimates the imaginary phallus.

The symbolic phallus, as the signifier of a lack, is a single signifier that has
different signifieds for different sexes. For example, the symbol for Phi or φ represents the missing symbolic phallus and the function of symbolic castration. The
latter function and symbol are what distribute the differences between the sexes.
In the case of masculinity, the signified for the phi signifier is φ or the imaginary
phallus, and in the case of femininity the signified is $-\varphi$. For masculinity, the loss
of the imaginary phallus that the boy is for the mother is lost under the phallic
function of symbolic castration.

However, such loss gives access to phallic jouissance for a man, and in the
case of femininity, to two forms of jouissance: phallic jouissance and feminine
jouissance outside the phallic order. In phallic jouissance, the $-\varphi$, or the lack of
the imaginary phallus in a female, results in a copula with the imaginary phallus
in a man (lose it so you can use it), while in feminine jouissance, the double loss
represented by the missing symbolic φ and imaginary phallus $-\varphi$ gives rise to
the square root of -1 ($\sqrt{-1}$) as the symbol for feminine jouissance that otherwise
lacks a signifier (two negatives when one of them is the $\sqrt{-1}$ equals the absence
of a signifier).

The $\sqrt{-1}$ is the symbol for a form of the third Other jouissance that is strictly
feminine. The experience of phallic jouissance for a woman always bears the risk
that the $-\varphi$ may be experienced as a deficit in relationship to masculinity, while
for a man, the presence of the φ, made possible by the phallic function of symbolic
castration, may appear to contradict the function of symbolic castration and place
a boy in a direct collision with his father. The boy must lose what he apparently
got from his father so that he can later use it. It is in the access to the cultural
order of the signifier that a man experiences his divided subjectivity and the loss
of the imaginary phallus required for the function of metaphor and symbolization.
In addition, a man must use the imaginary phallus under the bar of the Law and
in socially acceptable sexual activity. In the example of femininity, a double loss
of the imaginary phallus leads to both forms of sexual jouissance in a woman, as
well as access to the use of the signifier and the symbolic phallus in the cultural
Symbolic order.

The Sanskrit lingam (signifier) and yoni, for example, are different bodily signifieds for the signifier of a formless emptiness. In the Phi–phi relation, the -phi
represents an emptiness of absence, or the lack as deficit, while the $\sqrt{-1}$ represents the lack as the presence of a generative form of emptiness. Lacan again
engages Alcibiades's misrecognition much later in Seminar XXIII (1975–1976),
when he asks, how do we confuse an empty vessel or a bladder (yoni) for a lantern

(lingam), how do we mistake Socrates, or an empty container, for a phallic object? However, in the instance of feminine jouissance, emptiness appears gendered or "sexuated," while the emptiness of presence, or the Third jouissance, can also be *a*sexual, as in the case of the mystic and the jouissance of meaning. When Alcibiades misrecognizes Socrates, he is misrecognizing the Third jouissance for phallic jouissance. He mistakes Socrates's emptiness for the imaginary phallus.

When the clear mirror is opaque or obscure, the subject cannot see or symbolize things reflected in the empty mirror of Mind. Instead, the subject sees itself reflected in the world as a subjectively and linguistically perceived environment. However, when this subject perceives something wonderful in the Other, the Other is or represents a Clear Mirror. The Other is a wondrous emptiness or "no-thing." The various *objet a*'s (Lacan, 1966b; Moncayo, 2008) are all the forms of emptiness, of lack, Φ or $-\varphi$, and the "nothing" is an *objet a* in the Real.

Various imaginary *objet a*'s may appear in the Clear Mirror but are not the *objet a* in the Real, or the empty clear mirror itself.

> The eye is already a mirror. I shall say that the eye organizes the world in space. It reflects what, in the mirror, is reflection. To the most piercing eye, however, the reflection of what it carries of the world is visible in the eye that it sees in the mirror. To spell it right out, it has no need of two mirrors standing opposite one another for the infinite reflections of a mirror palace to be created.
>
> (Lacan, (1966/2014), p. 224)

Here, Lacan underscores how the eye organizes the world in space because the eye not only sees the Other behind the image of the subject, but also sees the subject reflected in the Other. The mirror of nature receives the forms of the subject within the forms of the world. At the same time, the eye of a subject as an organ and the I (*Je*) of the signifier also function as a mirror. The I of the signifier and the imaginary or visual eye of the ego reflect an infinite replication of images and signifiers. Within Lacanian theory, the reflection of images is Imaginary, while the clear mirror itself is both Real and Symbolic: symbolic because it is human made with numbers and signifiers in various ways, and Real because it is clear and empty.

While it is important not to confuse the clear mirror of Mind in Chan with the man-made object or cast mirror of Lacan's Imaginary, the man-made object is used by Lacan to represent a metaphoric image of the body of the subject. The Name, or a group of signifiers, symbolizes the image of the body. However, both Chan and Lacan approach an understanding of Mind that refers not only to human subjectivity or experience, in terms of images and signifiers, but to the emptiness of both that is shared with objects and things. The signifier is a signifier of a lack, and what things are outside the symbolic lacks a signifier. The clear mirror of mind refers to the emptiness symbolized by an empty mirror without images that allows a subject to see things as they are in their pristine purity. Mind as empty mirror accurately reflects the nature of things.

Mind as the vacuum is a default mode of human experience, and the vacuum is also a mode of functioning of matter at the level of the very small. Mind as vacuum, so to speak, refers to the amount of empty space that exists within the atom. It also refers to the empty space in-between thoughts, words, and signifiers. The outside of speech is determined by speech because a point of energetic condensation within a field of jouissance can also evolve into signification.

The clear Mirror is no-where or anything and everywhere. It is a state of Mind, a form of awareness beyond consciousness, as well as a polished and human-made reflective surface. Why do we say it is nowhere? Because it is not a thing or an object like a human-cast mirror. Could it be that we do not see it simply because it is too small for our perceptual apparatus?

The main point is that we do not see the mirror or the light in us although it is there. The true face is within the ordinary face, although ordinarily we do not see it. We cannot force the mirror to shine, nor can we deceive anyone about its shining, as Dogen said (1998, p. 214). The mirror shines of its own accord when the self-consciousness of the ego drops off or disappears.

Existence, with all its particularities and events, is one face of the Ancient Mirror. Freud's photo, taken by Moncayo at the Freud Museum in London (2015), shows a full moon that, in the photo, accidentally appeared reflected upon Freud's head. As a symbol for Freud's enlightened mind, or Freud as a face of the Ancestral mirror, this moon was not produced *per se* by the man-made camera and its flash that appears at the midpoint between Freud's photo and the statue of Avalokiteśvara, even though it would not have been produced without the technology and human labor of creating a photograph. It instead is a felicitous effect called lens flare that manifested at the time and location of Freud's head to produce an effect within a signifying context. This accident occasions the thought of how Freud's mind or clear mirror joins the ancestral mirror represented by the ancestral image of the full moon as a mirror. We cannot artificially and deliberately force the mirror to shine by means of technology, nor can we deceive anyone about its shining. The reflection in the ancestral clear mirror appears as an instantaneous form of "ex-sistence" in the here and now.

Now that we have discussed Lacan's mirrors in relationship to the Chan Ancient Mirror and Clear Mirror, we lay out some further implications of these connections between Buddhism and Lacan's thought. As we have seen, the forms of things or the entire universe are one face of the Ancient Mirror in Chan. The ancient mirror is not a thing, a visual apparatus, or a human-cast clear mirror with images. Mind as emptiness, although clear, is not an apparatus or a thing. If Mind were a particular thing, then it would not be clear. Because the Mind of a subject is clear, "It" can reflect the being of things as a clear bell resounding in all directions because the images and being of things are not obstructed. If a foreigner comes, a foreigner is reflected. When a Han comes, a Han is reflected. The mirror reflects both without discrimination (Dogen, 1200/1997, p. 245).

We might consider what happens if the Other walking toward you is a cast clear mirror with legs? Since the Other as mirror is empty, no reflections of the

Figure 11.1

Other appear in the subject. Both foreigner and Han disappear from the mirror of the subject, and the empty mirror of the Other is broken into speech or a thousand signifying pieces. If the empty mirror on legs walking toward you is not a metaphor for an enlightened Other or for what is Real or impossible in the Other, but is some form of a thing, automaton, Golem, computer, or robot, then the human being, the clear mirror, and the resonance of things between them would disappear. Conversely, we can understand how a wooden man, or stone woman, the ancient versions of a Golem, a computer, or a robot can also be metaphors to represent an egoless person who is in accord with or enlightened by the world. In this sense, a human being can become a computer, but a computer cannot become a human being. Every computer is made by and reflects a particular quality of humans, but a human is not a computer.

Earlier, we also saw how the Ancient Mirror as both "no-Mind" and the clear insubstantial Mind of a human can only appear in perception as the multiplicity of the entire universe. The entire universe becomes One bright pearl, or everything in the universe becomes One bright pearl or a formless jewel that is not a thing or a commodity. Somewhat paradoxically, an unblemished or spotless clear mirror as a thing separate from phenomena would be a flaw or scratch in the Clear Mirror since the Clear Mirror appears as potentiality in people's eyes and things alike. Although Mind is part of nature, and Buddha-nature, the clear empty Mind does not have a surface and is apparently immaterial. Mind does not have a surface since it is not a thing or an object (it is not the brain).

Is there a scientific explanation for a Mind that does not have a surface and is not a thing? If Mind is not an object, is it like a radiance or sound wave traveling in translucid space-time, and might waves or energy represent a mirror? Light is made up of tiny strings, packets, or photons, all mirrors of each other, and they travel as waves or particles. Atomic and subatomic particles and cells are made of tiny photons or mirrors shining in all directions. Photons are made of bosons, in contrast to fermions, which are the particles of most matter. Bosons are symmetrical and therefore can all fall into the lowest-energy orbital and somehow manage to exist at the same time, even as they are inexistent or immaterial for all practical purposes.

Hard material existence requires higher energy orbitals and increasingly larger "shells." Photons shine in the dark in the sense that if you do not observe them, they travel and shine unhindered, but if you observe them, as in self-consciousness, then they travel like particles and their faces no longer shine. Similarly, jouissance "perceives" and is perceived better when the cephalic eyes are not watching. All to say, our observations change what we see in such a way that particles mirror our assumptions, and what the phenomena would be without the act of observation remain unknown. Nature remains an empty mirror that cannot be boxed in, since any packet is simply reflected in the mirror. Without the human observations that make particles behave in predictable ways, bosons can also borrow energy from the future to cross through any barrier, and this means that at the level of the boson, particles and people could appear in multiple and faraway places at the same time and cannot be boxed in.

Humans have always looked at different patterns of photons that, thanks to the signifier, are mistaken for reality objects. This is an aspect of the opacity of the mirror. We do not see the reflective pattern or bundle of light that objects are. The signifier distracts us with the images of objects. Therefore, Chan offers a different modality of language to reach the light or find traces of light and illumination within letters themselves. Emptiness is the foundation of the statement. To see objects as unseen bundles of light and to perceive bundles of light becoming objects in the surfaceless mirror of Nature require the human Mind. When we perceive Mind in this clear way, as a bundle of light perceiving another bundle of light, then Nature becomes the Ancient Mirror, and Chan becomes you.

Given that the Clear Mirror appears as many things, or as a multiplicity rather than One special thing, person, or object, can the One also appear in a person? A person must not know that he or she knows he or she is the One to another, and not know when he or she is shining. For example, in the photo we discussed previously, Freud knows neither that he is a face of the ancestral clear mirror, nor that he is shining. As for Freud, the One appears in the person when the person is a unary trace of jouissance, a one that is zero, rather than a light bulb that can be turned on and off at will. The One is beyond the efforts or control of the subject.

By now, then, hopefully we have offered a deeper and more concrete sense of the ideas that: there is Mind as a Clear Mirror that is not a thing; and there is Mind in many things, or the One in the Many, or out of One, Many. It is interesting to note that things only have depth and dimension when they have a surface in the surface of the clear mirror (seen by human eyes). When you have a surface, then you also know an object's Real depth. This is where Lacan exercised some caution with defining psychoanalysis as a "depth psychology." While the reference is partially justified, for certainly the unconscious and Mind are deep, the Unconscious also manifests on the surface of speech and consciousness. Truth is staring us in the face.

The Chinese language already contains many of the ideas we have been exploring in this section. Many psychological terms in Chinese language and culture have been derived from the influence of Chan Buddhism and Mahayana psychology into the language and culture over the centuries. Chinese language, and Chan Buddhism in turn influenced the cultures of Korea and Japan (where Chan is known as *Seon* and Zen, respectively). We have mentioned that Chan is a blend of *Shi* and *Dao* and Confucian thought, and in this sense Chan studies include all three. The convergence of these three streams can be said to be a defining characteristic of traditional Chinese culture.

Chan was how Buddhism became Chinese and was integrated into everyday life. From *Baizhang*'s "A Day of Not Working, is a Day of Not Eating," to *Chao Chou*'s "Everyday Life is the Way," Chan became a non-dual path inclusive of Buddhas and ordinary people. The Mahayana Vimalakirti Sutra featured a lay Buddha, and this made this sutra very popular in China.

The Chinese term for the *Unconscious* is 无意识 *Wúyìshí. Wú* (无 or 無) signifies not to have, no, none, not, to lack; and *yishi* is consciousness. However, Lacan's Real unconscious means more *Wú-juézhī*, or awareness of Wú, meaning awareness of the nonconscious or the Real unconscious. In our reading, *Wú-juézhī*, or awareness of *Wú*, does not mean unawareness because *Wú* is not a binary negation. *Wúyìshí* means unconscious but also as a unary negation means consciousness of the repressed unconscious. Consciousness recognizes or affirms what has been repressed and is not a simple negation of it. *Wú-juézhī* in turn as a unary negation does not mean unconscious as unawareness, but rather signifies non-dual awareness of the Real unconscious. In sum, the Chinese term for the Freudian *unconscious*, *Wúyìshí*, means awareness of the repressed as *Wú*, while the Chinese term for the Real unconscious means more *Wú-juézhī* or awareness of the Real unconscious as *Wú*.

Wúyìshí is also related to 意识到"无" or *Yì shí dào wú*, meaning awareness or realizing (认识) the place or way of lack or emptiness or pure desire without cling-ing, and letting go and letting be (放下). This corresponds to Lacan's "*L'insu qui sait*" (the unknown that knows about lack or emptiness), rather than what Freud called consciousness (Pcs-Cs. system). The unknown here refers to an awareness without self-consciousness that corresponds to Freud's Pcpt-Cs. system that does not keep any memories or registrations, and in this way, awareness has a quality of truth in the sense of Lethes or forgetting.

In the practice of analysis, *Wú-juézhī* or *Wú* awareness represents those moments of insight and realization brought about by the signifier functioning as a pointer or index of jouissance. Since jouissance has at least equivalence with the signifier in this instance, the psyche here functions with the signifier but also outside the signifier, and, therefore, conscious memory and registration may or may not be there. In other words, when the subject has an epiphany in analysis, this epiphany is in synchronic time but may not be remembered in diachronic memory over time. The subject will have to re-immerse himself or herself in the experience of the *gong'an* (*koan*) moment in analysis where awareness of *Wú* and the experience of a liberating jouissance may appear once again.

Focusing on the linguistic significance of Wu in the Chinese language allows us to further appreciate that Chan, although containing a rich and profound Mahayana psychology, is itself neither a psychology, nor a religion, nor a philosophy. When asked to say something deep about the Dharma, *Chou Chu* answered: "What part of the depth do you want me to talk about, the 8 of 8 or the 4 of 4?" The response, on first blush, seems incomprehensible. But taken in context, it makes perfect sense: you want me to talk about being at a depth of eight feet while speaking with you at the surface of the experience of What, "This"? I can see the depth in the sur-face of your face. To answer something deep, you go to the surface of the question.

This brings us nicely back to our previous discussion of "Just This." The surfaceless mirror of Nature can only be the Ancient mirror when seen with the clear eye of "Just This." "Just This" is a better signifier than Mind here because referring to "Just This" as "Mind" runs the risk of objectifying "Just This." Nature and Mind or Mind and Nature are the two faces of the Ancient Mirror realized by the Clear Mirror of Mind. In other words, the clear uncast mirror or Mind encounters the opaque or surfaceless mirror in things and realizes the beauty of things and their opacity when seen in the Clear Mirror. Although the Clear Mirror is empty and appears in present time as something inexistent, ineffable, or immaterial (Mind), when it appears in space-time and in matter that contains or is time, then the Clear Mirror is the Ancient mirror. The mind-moon that appeared in Freud's head as an ancient or ancestral mirror represents the inexistent or immaterial luminous mind as "This" instantaneous existence appearing in space-time. Like this mind-moon, Buddha is the name of now and of the body of awareness and jouissance, and not of prior names or ancestors that no longer live among us or in us, or who no longer are who we thought they were. Buddha is the name of the ancestor or the Ancestral Mirror as a clear mirror in the here and now of space-time.

The play of language between English and French, as well, avails us of further insight. The eye is also the I and the I is *Je* in French. The eye sees through the I or *Je* of the signifier. *Je* in Lacanian theory stands for the signifier or for how the signifier structures the field of vision. The imaginary eye of visual perception is the ideal ego or the me (*moi* in French) that sees through the "lens" of the *objet a* of fantasy and desire. In addition, the eye as an organ cannot see without signifiers and corresponding visual objects.

Three forms of seeing images or perceiving through the senses are raised by this cluster of English and French words. First, through signifiers ("wow, what a beautiful flower"); second, through imaginary fantasies and desires for the object ("wow, what a beautiful woman"); and third, through "Just This." The first two forms comprise what we ordinarily refer to as objective visual images of objects through a code of signifiers and numbers. However, "Just this" refers to pure seeing or hearing of the object's singularity, hearing the ringing in the ears, ringing is ringing, and objects are ringing, without piling on additional descriptions. It also refers to a resonance of jouissance with the object as seen and heard, for example, in the purring of a cat.

Jouissance is the music that the subjective cord of the subject plays in response to the Third Other jouissance. "Just this" is the subject of the Real, or the right and inheritance of beings to be Buddha, or the ancestral mirror of ancestors, despite or because of their lack and imperfections. "Even those things from which flaws are produced are also the Ancient Mirror" (Dogen, 1998a, p. 251). The blunders and slips of the Clear Mirror are the result of the Ancient Mirror "having too much to do."

The form of seeing through signifiers is also exemplified by technology (the Hubble telescope, for example, used for the image in Figure 11.2), praxis or labor, and the clear "eye" of the fabricated mirror. These three forms allow alternative ways to see the outer and inner worlds otherwise unavailable through the senses. The Hubble telescope functions like a larger clear cast mirror constructed, thanks to advancements in physics and mathematics: for the outer universe, what we see through the telescope are in fact objects from the past that no longer exist as we see them through a telescope. A telescope does not appear as a clear mirror in the present moment (because time is distorted by the speed of light, and you do not actually see how celestial objects are at the time of the observation). Thus, strictly speaking, the clear mirror is Mind and not an instrument or a fabricated mirror.

Consider, as well, the example of a ceramic tile that is a natural mirror without having the surface of a mirror, and is neither a cast clear mirror, nor the clear mirror of Mind. As a particular opaque object, a tile is a mirror made of sand and by itself is either meaningless or has a purely utilitarian function. But if a subject practices, polishes, and labors with the tile in interdependence (many elements and forms of human labor contribute to the making of a tile), then the clarity of the insubstantial Mind evoked in the subject also turns the tile into a surfaceless mirror that is also a clear mirror.

If the human Mind or the tile is not turned into an unfabricated clear mirror, then the tile remains a thing rather than a "no-thing," a particular and meaningless piece of waste, like the plastic destroying our oceans. If the tile is not "practiced" or worked with, then the tile remains an opaque object (surfaceless mirror) of no value to a subject. Conversely, when the tile is singularly practiced and polished, and becomes Mind, then the entire universe is a bright pearl that represents the face of the Ancient mirror. In the image in Figure 11.2, we see the bright mirror as a bright pearl or the form that a polished tile takes, both large and small in dimension, that as a concentrated field of luminosity, is structurally like the development of "cephalic eyes."

Indeed, this image depicts how the face of the Ancient Mirror is represented by a round mirror. A polished tile via praxis or labor represents the mirror of nature as the clear mirror of Mind concretely visualized as an elliptical image of the universe. A tile as an opaque or unpolished man-made object can be seen as the Ancient Mirror, but only by working through a form of thinking distorted by imaginary reflections and preconceptions. For Lacan, the imaginary eye is a

Figure 11.2

natural mirror rather than a clear mirror, thus leading to imaginary and fantasized forms of thinking, that not only are inevitable, but can also be transformed within the knot into the creative imagination. The creative imagination allows a subject to "see" where the cephalic imaginary cannot.

This Ancestral Mirror, as appearing in the tile, that has neither a front nor back, that is neither knowledge nor instrument, and that is our right and proper inheritance, represents the emptiness and heart in things. Myriad forms carry the Ancient Mirror in their backs (or heads). But the Ancient Mirror is not determined by the many forms in which it is carried. The Ancient Mirror represents humanity (Ren) or Buddha. It is humans who fabricate mirrors and see the clear mirror of Mind in the ancient mirror that forms carry on their backs. Dogen asks us to contemplate the fact that it is humans who call apes, apes. Does this imply that we are the orange, red-faced apes? Can we discover whether this is true or false? Just 700 years after Dogen, Darwin and an archaeological reading of fossil records show that, indeed, we are the orange, red-faced apes, our closest living relatives are chimpanzees, and our lineage split from theirs about seven million years ago.

This intersection between Dogen's question about the red-faced ape and Darwin's taxonomic system is an example of how, if the world is not reflected in the clear and Ancient Mirror of thought, and we use thinking to project onto the outside world, our thinking comes back to us from the forms of the world reflected in the surfaceless mirror. We mistake this for objectivity. Lacan described this phenomenon with the term "*objetality*." On the one hand, *objetality* refers to the part played by the ordinary human imaginary and fantasy in perception. On the other hand, neologism *objetality* can also refer to the positive creative force of a symbolized human imagination writ large.

In imaginary thinking, the world is infinite and uncountable, but this form of natural infinity in the opaque mirror is not grounded in zero or the null set present in all sets and numbers. The clear mirror requires the numbers 0 and 1. The number 1 is for the unified body image in the mirror, and 0 stands for the empty mirror background of the image.

The fact that the body image is only a consistent image of the body without material existence other than as a mental reflection makes it possible for the body image to be replaced by the specular images of siblings and friends that function as alter ego to the ideal ego or body image of a subject. An entire material body cannot occupy another material body but a mental image of another body through imaginary identification can occupy the body and identity of a subject. The subject now thinks of another body image rather than his or her own, and his or her ego identity becomes displaced: "I am another" who is not lacking. This metonymical thinking through imaginary identification with the alter ego is how the subject attempts to recover the objects of desire that have been lost.

There is a multiplicity of thought and a multiplicity of thinking. The multiplicity of thought refers to how the forms and activities of nature are reflected in the human mirror of mind without imaginary reflections. How a bird flies or reproduces represents the "thought" of nature reflected in the human empty mirror.

In multifarious thinking, and "As soon as there is an eye and a mirror, the infinite recursion of inter-reflected images is produced" (Lacan, 1963/2014, p. 224), things are opaque, and their structural relations are not realized.

In contrast, the infinity that is everywhere as a bright pearl (the zero or 0 in the thing), is reflected as a pure thought in the clear mirror of Mind. True objectivity requires the Real of thought in the clear mirror. The Real of thought is how non-thought, emptiness, or a different form of jouissance goes into thought, and how the forms of nature are reflected in the clear mirror of thought. The Real of thought is not a special thought-form, identity, or series reflected in the empty mirror. It is a pure thought form that is the mental equivalent of the "objective" object, as well as a thought in the mind of a subject.

The mirror in nature that Lacan speaks of, where everything can be reflected as a fabrication or artifice of the human mind, can function both as an imaginary and symbolic representation. For humans, nature is an opaque mirror without the human Mind. Nature here represents the object world of need and desire more than the reality of things the way they are. The human Mind is not simply a cultural fabrication but an aspect of human and Buddha-nature. Buddha-nature is a metaphor for the Ancient Mirror that is more than human and resides in the clear mirror of every human being. However, every human being also has images of nature, as imaginary thinking projected onto nature without the clear mirror of Mind. When humans polish the mirror of nature, then the clear mirror is also the Ancient Mirror.

Animism represents a time when people felt persecuted and enlightened by nature and believed that nature was a receptacle for the human spirit. Religion and then *techne* and modern science would subsequently disenchant nature of this belief. In the name of knowing nature in a more pure and scientific form, without projection or superstition, science (developed especially under the historic dominance of modern capitalism) has also enabled human destruction of life on a massive scale and proliferated discord in the ways of nature, which made humans and civilization possible in the first place.

The negative consequences of science and modern disenchantment suggest that the magic associated with animism was not necessarily false, which is different from saying that it was true. The truth approached by animism is especially shown, for example, in Pantheism, which is the belief that humans can participate in the immanent divinity of the Universe without the mediation of traditional religious institutions. Pantheism resolves the contradiction between science and animism by discovering the mind or spirit of G-d within the Universe itself. In fact, scientists such as Einstein and Dirac were Pantheists. Taoism, as an alternative example, moves beyond Pantheism into a panentheistic belief system based on the idea that there is something beyond Nature akin to what Lacan develops as the Real, or the world of mathematics as laid out by Plato. Buddhism, and Chan Buddhism in particular, is nontheistic.

Pantheism expresses an informed love of nature, and because of this, partially rejects the critique of animism and the archaic mentality linked to the modern disenchantment of nature associated with science and technology. Although *techne*, as a form of instrumental reason, works for the survival of the species, if not balanced by other forms of Aristotelian rationality, it also destroys natural habitats and the very atmosphere humans depend on.

This pantheistic approach to animism and science is consistent with the distinction that Lacan makes between myth as an archaic animistic and imaginary fantasy grafted upon the mathematical Real attempting to supplant it (Lacan's first Real) and myth as the intersection between the Symbolic, language, and the Real. In the latter case, myth may be saying something true about the Real that cannot be said any other way. From this perspective, we must re-enchant nature and polish tiles into panentheistic clear Mirrors contained within living human eyes (Pantheism). Otherwise, as far as the solar system is concerned, or the universe as we know it so far, the earth could just as well be the surface of Mars or Venus with no oxygen or water to speak of.

Chapter 12

The One, the Many, and *Kuan-yin*

An animistic world represents how humans confuse the world with thinking that does not have a way of transforming ideas into symbolic thoughts in accord with reality. Things are not reflected in thought. Rather, thinking is reflected in the opaque surface of things, and thinking, in turn, can become displaced and multifarious. A natural resource becomes an opaque thing, a commodity, or a fetish that reflects our own greed or need as human beings.

In contrast, Chan practice, psychoanalysis, or science offers ways to see the world reflected in pure thought or in the clear mirror of mind, at which point the world as the Ancient Mirror appears as it is, or as things are from the perspective of both form and emptiness: "Just This." Similarly, in psychoanalysis, when imaginary thinking and desire are symbolized in speech in the personal experience of analysis, thinking becomes pure thought that reflects the world in the clear mirror, and thus, an experience of "Just This."

> This remark about the infinite deployment of inter-reflected images, which are produced once there is an eye and a mirror, is not here simply for the ingeniousness of the remark, but on the contrary to bring us back to the privileged point which is at the origin, which is the same as the one in which there is bound up the original difficulty of arithmetic, the foundation of the one and the zero. The one image, the one which is made in the eye, I mean the one that you can see in the pupil, requires from the beginning of this development a correlate which for its part is not an image at all.
>
> (Lacan, 08.05.63 XVII 155, trans. by Gallagher)

This "correlate" that is "not an image" is a so-called real object. However, an object is also an image, and so the only difference between an image and a real object is the signifier or the name of the object. Once the object is apprehended as a signifier, then another dimension of the object opens beyond the image and the signifier. This is the object as *das Ding* that functions as an undetermined "no-thing" that mirrors and supports the world. This object, or image that is not an image, is neither a letter nor an algorithm, but a form of Real jouissance. Emptiness or the lack as a form of jouissance functions as a form of ease with a principle of uncertainty,

DOI: 10.4324/9781003198765-12

impermanence, or unknowing through which decisions can be made, even in the absence of causal knowledge and certainty. The absence of causal understanding regarding certain truths of desire/jouissance, or causality in the form of a gap or incompleteness as formulated by Gödel, is precisely what establishes the consistency of Mind as a symbolic or linguistic representational order.

The "true" as a half-truth at the level of representation emerges here as a certain correspondence between image or proposition and real object. In contrast, truth proper in the Real refers to the jouissance that, from outside of the Symbolic and the Imaginary, and yet within the Borromean knot, supports and/or organizes the multiplicity contained within symbolic structure.

Lacan draws a connection between these two forms of truth (truth as jouissance and truth as representation) and the Buddha as constituted within a dialectic of the One and the Many. Like the monad, linked not isolated, the Buddha is a real One and, at the same time, many Ones, insofar as every human has the potential to realize their Buddha-nature as a singular and intimate experience. The One refers to how the Real always returns to the same place or "no-place" of jouissance, while the Many refers not only to the fact that there can be many Buddhas, but that such Buddhas must be named according to the logic of the signifier, with its metaphors and metonymic displacements.

The dialectic between the One and the Many is also reflected in the relationship between Buddhas and bodhisattvas. Outside the imaginary self-other duality, and beyond a hierarchical relation, bodhisattvas are Buddhas-to-be, and Buddhas can manifest as bodhisattvas. Their relation is not based on status, but rather, mutual respect between beings: teacher and student, Buddhas and bodhisattvas, and crucially, analysts and analysands. Lacan's incorporation of Buddhist thought and practice provides us with a fresh and unique perspective on the position of the analyst, insofar as it is of One and Many, instead of someone or another. The analyst is a symbolic character that interprets signifiers linked to unconscious fantasies, and at the same time is a Real subject with a form of subjective jouissance (equanimity with respect to love and hate in the transference) that supports the analyst's authority and interpretive function.

> If the surface of the mirror is not there to support the world, it is not because nothing reflects this world, it is not because the world vanishes with the absence of the subject, it is properly what I said in my first formula: it is that nothing is reflected; before reflection, there is a one which contains multiplicity.
>
> (idem, p. 224)

The One that contains multiplicity refers not to the one cast mirror with reflections, but to the O-ne that is the zero represented by the emptiness of the mirror without reflections. The mirror itself is empty without reflections, but because of its absence of reflection or not having its own self or reflection can reflect the images, and upon the images that appear before it. Reflection here means both image and thinking. The empty mirror is both a cast mirror and a representation for the emptiness of a Real subject. The world is sustained by the emptiness of the subject as a subject rather than by the absence of a human subject.

Lacan believes Buddhas are bodhisattvas that quickly create a luminous void within the designation Buddha-to-be or almost Buddha. The void in this case is not just the void that Buddha represents, but a symbolic lack of being (Buddha) or of entering Nirvana, which is generated by Buddha as bodhisattva who, in the Mahayana tradition, stays in the world of beings and suffering. The Buddha as bodhisattva is one that although having left the world, has not succeeded in becoming indifferent to the suffering of the world or humanity (a lack of indifference toward the Other). In this case, Buddha as bodhisattva guarantees that all beings irrespective of class, status, race, illness, or defect are the Buddha-nature. Buddha as bodhisattva is a good representation of the beneficence of a structural lack-in-the-Other ($\varnothing$), or the compassionate aspect of the Buddha that stays in the world and helps all beings realize enlightenment. Just like there are many Buddhas, there are several great bodhisattvas, each with a thousand helpful arms.

> But in order to make you understand what I mean as regards this One which is not mono but poly, all in the plural – I will simply show you what you can see at Kamakura – it is the work of a sculptor whose name is well known; Kamakura is from the end of the 12th century – it is Buddha represented, materially represented by a statue three meters high, and materially represented by a thousand others.
>
> (idem)

At the same time, Lacan clarifies that:

> The monotheism/polytheism opposition might not be such a clear-cut thing as you habitually imagine it to be, because the thousand and one statues standing there are all identically the same Buddha. For the thousand and one statues which are there are all properly and identically the same Buddha.
>
> (idem)

Lacan also goes on to point out that although the many are all the same Buddha, the Buddha, by right, is also you, or each real subject.

> Besides, by right, each one of you is a Buddha, I say by right because for particular reasons you may have been thrown into the world with some defect which may constitute a more or less irreducible obstacle to gaining access to it.
>
> (idem, p. 156)

Lacan says "by right" to underscore that One does not have to be perfect to be Buddha. To be born and "thrown into the world" with some defect only makes the lack or the deficit function as a barrier or obstacle that hastens the maturation of the subject as Buddha. Symbolic lack or impermanence only *appears* to be a barrier or a Real obstacle. An imaginary bodily defect symbolized as a symbolic lack can be an access point to the Real.

> I told you what a Buddha was. It is not absolutely speaking a God, it is a bodhisattva, which means to go quickly and create a void, as I might say, an almost Buddha. It would be completely a Buddha if precisely it was not there; but since it is there, and under this multiplied form, which has demanded, as you see, a lot of trouble, this is only the image of the trouble that he for his part takes to be there. He is there for you.
>
> (idem)

The bodhisattva takes the trouble of being there for you, as Lacan says, perhaps not unlike the analyst, or the good shepherd of Christianity, or the father who pays a price to raise and help the children. Lacan, despite rejecting the idea that psychoanalysis is anything like re-parenting or pastoral counseling in the sense of the orientation of souls, also believed that the analyst had to make three payments in the exercise of the analytical function. "Lacan tells us that the analyst is paid for his or her own personal payments that are required as part of the analytical function. The analyst pays not only with his or her professional qualifications, but with something of his or her own personal and subjective being, a subjective loss within his or her own person" (Moncayo, 2021, p. 165).

"More than being paid for their knowledge and expertise, analysts are in fact paid for strategically losing the position of the subject supposed to know. Analysts lose the knowledge that otherwise they would be paid for. They are paid for the loss of the claim to knowledge rather than for its use. And analysts achieve this by employing the "third ear" or what Lacan calls *J'ouis-sense* (hearing more than listening)" (idem).

> He is a Buddha who has not yet succeeded in disinteresting himself, no doubt because of one of these obstacles to which I alluded earlier, to disinterest himself in the salvation of humanity. That is the reason why, if you are Buddhists, you prostrate yourself before this sumptuous gathering. It is because in effect you owe, I think, recognition to the unity which has troubled itself in such a great number to remain within range of bringing you help. For there is also said – the iconography enumerates it – the cases in which they will bring you help.
>
> (idem)

Lacan is gesturing to a particular bodhisattva in question in the statues he observes: Avalokiteśvara. Avalokiteśvara is the Sanskrit name for the bodhisattva that hears (*J'ouis-Sense*) the cries, suffering, and mood of the world. Avalokiteśvara is also known as *Kuan-yin* or *Kuan-shih-yin* in China, and *Kannon* in Japan. Kuan-yin can be either a masculine or a feminine figure but is more commonly rendered as a feminine representation of the Buddha's compassionate wisdom.

Lacan's elaborations in Seminar XX on feminine sexuality can extend our understanding of *Kuan-yin*'s feminine form. Feminine jouissance and the jouissance of the "mystic" are two of the forms of the Third jouissance that Lacan mentions in Seminar XX. Of course, Lacan's reference to "mysticism" should not be confused as a Buddhist term since mysticism is typically otherworldly, while Buddhism is focused on this world. Mystical realism is another way, too, to approach Lacan's discussion of "Woman" as one of the names of the NoF as a function. Lacan writes "name" here with a lower case to signify plurality, while at the same time, one of the names, "Woman," far from indicating a sociological designation of gender, can be read as the proper address for femininity as a singularity and a form of (feminine) jouissance.

Kuan-yin as an object, where feminine sexuality and meditation practice meet, offers a new way of thinking about the *objet a* where two forms of the Third jouissance (the feminine and the mystic) meet. We might say that *Kuan-yin*, as both a Buddhist and Lacanian object, is "*Wu*-man." "*Wu*-man" designates a symbolically castrated imaginary phallus or "no man." For a woman, "not man" leads to feminine jouissance; while for a man, "not imaginary man" results in a certified symbolic phallus and a Third jouissance beyond phallic jouissance.

As an object representing meditation practice, the proper name *Kuan-yin*, meaning "like the wheel of desires," is very fitting. Through meditation, *Kuan-yin* as the wheel of desires is transformed into a representation of the wheel of Nirvana. The question of *Kuan-yin*'s sexual ambiguity for Lacan addresses the degree to which she is or is not an object of desire, and at the same time represents the symbolic desire of the mother for the child as a subject, rather than as her narcissistic object. *Kuan-yin* as a feminine figure provokes contemplation of the *objet a* as cause of the movement of the wheel of desire, and its transformation into a missing or lacking object, which in turn manifests the experience of emptiness that turns the wheel of Nirvana.

Here is where we arrive at a most fascinating discussion by Lacan of the function of the eye and the gaze in the statue, which further illuminates the idea of feminine sexuality as "*Wu*-man":

> If you still need other details, you may notice that there is no opening of the eyes in this statue. Now, the Buddhist statues always have eyes that one cannot call shut, but half-shut, because it's a way of poising the eyes that is only arrived at by learning, namely, a lowered eyelid that only lets show a line of the white and an edge of the pupil. All the statues of Buddha are made like that.

> (idem, p. 228)

Kuan-yin's half-shut eyes beg the question of the gaze and its relationship to both a surfaceless mirror and a clear mirror of Mind, as discussed in the previous chapter.

Lacan observes that the physical rubbing of the statue's eyes over the centuries has erased the opening of the eye, so that effectively, the Buddha is metaphorically blind, or is looking at a blank screen or wall rather than the forms of the world. Lacan also points out the ordinary features of the eyes in Buddhist statues, as if they had not been erased through repeated rubbing. However, in this description, he does not mention that "half-shut" eyes represent elements of the meditation posture and instead focuses on the structure of a cut and an opening that allows for an object to circulate between the inside and outside of a subject.

Indeed, Zen or Chan meditation can be described as the activity of a cut-out swinging door between inside and outside (a good metaphor for the subject of jouissance and the circulation of signifiers). The so-called door of perception is a cut that mediates between inside and outside. The cut can be a cut in sound or the lips and nose that facilitate and accentuate the circulation of air or the breath, as well as cuts within the word and with the phallic signifier as a pointer, hole puncher, or marks on paper, membranes, metals, and sound waves. Inspiration (as both inhalation and inspiration), exhalation, aspiration, and transmission.

> Let's not forget that at an altogether different level, the level of the signifying articulation, at the level of the most fundamental phonemes, those most firmly bound to the cut (O A), the consonantal elements of the phoneme, are, as regards their most basal stock, essentially modulated at the level of the lips.
>
> (idem, p. 232)

So, too, can this modulation of the cut be achieved with the eyes. The eyes are kept open in Buddhist meditation because the Buddha does not close their eyes to the world. Closed eyes in Hindu meditation represent a withdrawal from the world into inner spiritual realms or states. Through the cut, or half-shut eyes, there is a flow of jouissance between the Real and the reality of the signifier or ordinary life. This is what the eye as a cut, as an anatomical feature of the eye, as a beautiful curve or line, allows and realizes.

But *Kuan-yin*'s eyes have been eroded down after so many years of touching and rubbing the statue's eyes. Erased eyes at this moment refers to the "third eye" featured in many Buddhist statues that represents the "inexistence" of what one sees with the ordinary eyes of the everyday imaginary. While ordinary imaginary eyes distort reality or "vision," we hear through the Symbolic signifier, or the Real of jouissance, which represents a form of doctoral blindness or a non-seeing that is true seeing or true hearing. If we take the erased eyes as the symbolic gaze, *Kuan-yin* represents, too, the function of the third ear of "*J'ouis-Sense*" in psychoanalysis.

To prevent the analysand from telling the analyst only what he or she wants him or her to know, or what the analysand thinks the analyst wants to hear, the analytical arrangement is not face-to-face. The analyst behind the couch, the computer screen, or on the phone dislocates the illusions of imaginary face-to-face recognition to see with something other than the imaginary. This is the structural reason for the use of the couch rather than thinking that the only reason for the couch is the capriciousness, idiosyncrasies, or personal likes and dislikes of Freud, who could not stand being looked at for hours on end.

The rubbing of *Kuan-yin*'s eyes for Lacan is proof that she represents an object of desire for nuns and monks. *Kuan-yin*, as an object of desire, may represent something like what Socrates represented for Alcibiades, that is, a woman's or a *Wu*-man's emptiness or inexistence, an *objet a* in the Real. At the same time, Lacan uses the reference to Socrates in the Symposium as a clinical indication for the position of the analyst as the receptacle of transference love. Transference love refers to how love manifests in the transference relationship via an imaginary *objet a*, while love's transference refers to the transference that takes place in any love relation. *Kuan-yin* perceived and desired (or not) as an imaginary *objet a* would be an Eastern feminine reference for the position of the analyst as a woman (*Wu*-man).

Transference to the analyst sitting behind the couch, the screen, or at the other end of the phone takes place through something like the rubbing of Avalokiteśvara's eyes. The analysand metaphorically rubs the analyst's eyes as *objet a*, where rubbing represents the activity of extracting enjoyment and pain from relating to the analyst or the Other of the Unconscious. Transference love as a form of "frotteurism," from the French verb *frotter*, meaning "to rub," can be understood alongside the breast that is metaphorically sucked, or the genitals rubbed in sexual activity.

Perhaps it is more accurate to say that the rubbing of signifiers itself represents the action of the jouissance subtly produced in an analysis and is a central aspect of the therapeutic effect of psychoanalytical treatment. The drive, like space-time, has the topological structure of a rubber sheet. Rubbing is the activity of the rubber band that turns the *objet a* into "rub-bish," or an object of waste for possible recycling. Recycling, as a metaphor for the analytic process, transforms an object of waste into the mirror of Nature seen by a clear mirror of mind. A new analytic object in the surface of the clear mirror involved in analysis shines. At this point, the thing in the Real represents a "packet" of light shining in the mirror of Nature, the surface of Nature as a clear mirror, and the clear mirror of Mind, all at once.

Chapter 13

Clinical Dream Example

Analysand's Dream

I was in my bed and tried hard to ask Siri to turn on my nightstand lamp on, but it just didn't work. Even though Siri responded to me "OK, it's on" the way she usually speaks after turning on the lamp, the lamp was still off. I realized that maybe Siri turned the bed lamp on and not the one here in my parents' apartment. I found I had no other way to turn on the light, and I could only count on Siri to turn it on. I took out my cellphone to check the background setting for Siri and tried to turn the lamp on via my cellphone. I found my cellphone was playing an introduction of a suspense thriller or horror movie.

There was dim light from the window in my room and I found I was in the bed in our old apartment where I lived with my parents and my mother's foster parents when I was in elementary school and middle school. My mother had been raised by her biological parents until she was sent away at age 15. She did not feel loved and desired by her parents or husband. Behind my bed was the balcony where I found a lot of clothes and thick sheets hung out to dry. I tried to move them aside, hoping the light from outside could get into my bedroom, only to the find the light outside looked like the dim light from that suspense thriller movie. I heard screaming from my bed and found my former wife was there. I tried to comfort her by hugging her and telling her "Don't be afraid, don't be afraid."

In the next scene, I was in my therapeutic group where the two leaders, a married couple, were commenting on one of the participants who had just said that he felt a lot of fear. Mr. So-and-So (the male therapist) said: Because he doesn't have a cohesive personality, he cannot condense his feeling to identify and articulate what on earth scared him. In contrast to the group participant in the dream, I was sacred/scared (slip of the tongue) of recounting a lot of tiny little unrelated insignificant things. For example, feeling that a hotel room was spooky; or a dark ventilation hole/hold (slip) was scary; or the feeling of someone behind him, etc. If I could condense my feeling, I might be able to dig deeper to see what's beneath all these fears.

I encouraged myself to be brave and face my fear. I was quite sure that I was in my bed in my current bedroom where behind my bed is just a wall. But I just felt

DOI: 10.4324/9781003198765-13

that behind me, behind my bed was a balcony, and a big eye was staring at me, at my back. I was afraid.

Associations

When asked for associations, the analysand said, "The big eye staring at me reminded me of a phobia I once had when I was five." On the way to visiting maternal grandparents, and crossing a road, there was an advertisement for a brand that showed a hanging silk cloth with a cut in it, and from which the eye of a woman appeared staring at him. He was scared by this eye he saw on the billboard. He associated the woman's eye peeping through a crevasse or cut in the right top corner of the silk material with an eye inside the mother's vagina that could suck all of him up.

This is a compelling representation of the example of anxiety provided by Lacan in his Seminar on Anxiety. It is the appearance of the *objet a*, where a lack, absence, or emptiness should be, that triggers anxiety. Anxiety is the signal of something that is outside the signifier and that appears in the place where the phallus is missing. The lack in the (m)Other (or the question "What does the Other want from me?") is what triggers anxiety. In addition, the dream shows how a childhood phobia, as an example of childhood neurosis, can have a lasting influence in a person's life.

He also associated his dream with what a psychoanalyst said in China about the mother as "holy mother," "castrating bitch," and "whore." In Lacanian theory, we would say that the holy mother is Symbolic, while the so-called bitch and whore are versions of the Imaginary mother. Such first jouissance could be comforting or engulfing and persecutory. However, object relations theory, and the worldwide psychoanalysis it represents, cannot interpret beyond this first jouissance without a concept of the NoF, the phallus, or symbolic castration. By contrast, the Real mother as the archaic body of the mother is the thing or *das Ding*, or the eyes through which we interpret the world as animated by a shared jouissance between subject and object (as seen in the example of petting a purring cat).

In a visit to Tibet, and prior to beginning analysis, the analysand tattooed a pair of eyes of Buddha on his back. Here the eyes of his father "have his back," so to speak. The gaze of the symbolic father protects him from the mother's eye, identified with an imaginary phallus. In addition, the gaze symbolizes and renders benevolent the lack or emptiness in the mother. The gaze (imaginary *objet a*) coming through the analysand's window in the dream, in this case, represents the imaginary phallus that appears in the mother where the phallus is missing.

In the dream, the imaginary gaze of the (m)Other functions as an index of an unbearable emotional life experience of imaginary castration that the mind bears through the dream-work. The persecutory eye in the dream is staring at his back or is "on his back" rather than "having his back." The mother's eye in the place where her sex or an absence should be supersedes the calming effect of the father's gaze, or the gaze of his father could not replace his mother's eye qua imaginary phallus. With the supplement of the tattoo, the gaze of the symbolic father now "has his back" and protects him from the dangers he cannot see.

Family and Oedipal structure: the analysand's father said to him that his mother was not attractive to him. The mother told the analysand that she did not want to have sex with his father because he was dirty and smelly and that the analysand, as her son, was more important to her than his father. When his mother left a rose in his room, the analysand moved it to his father's desk and subsequently found the rose on the kitchen table. According to Lacan's seminar on the object relation, we might read this Oedipal situation as one in which there is no real father because the father did not desire the mother and the marriage for him was simply a good arrangement. At the same time, the analysand did have a symbolic father because the father did recognize him and provided a modicum of separation from the mother. It is this modicum that is at issue. Although there is enough separation to make him neurotic rather than perverse, it was not enough to prevent him from feeling engulfed or seduced by the mother, however much he enjoyed the intimacy and exclusivity he had with her, especially in childhood.

The analysand reported another dream where he was at the barber shop watching a TV screen while his hair was being cut. Paradoxically, however, because he had a helmet on, they could not cut his hair. All the while, he watched on TV a monk kill a monster or the ghost of a beautiful lady who was a demon that would suck all the energy out of a man. One drop of semen equals ten drops of blood, the analysand explained. In this dream, the helmet protecting the head protected the head of the phallus from a woman. This corresponds to the analysand's fear of being sucked into the womb and being eaten and digested by the vagina *dentata* (fantasy that the womb and the stomach are connected).

Appendix
The Practice of Thinking Non-thinking or Thinking/Meditating with the Body of the Third Jouissance

In *zazen*, or sitting (*zuo*) Chan, we suspend our usual activities, both mental and physical, and focus on the understanding of posture, breathing, and silence in the present moment. We look at a blank wall instead of the ordinary seeing of objects. Our usual thoughts, sensations, and feelings are the product/result of our past actions and are directed to some future goal, wish, or idea. *Zuo chan* is the practice of letting go of this goal-directed thinking, feeling, or sensation. In sitting Chan, we cultivate calm, flexible, or soft mind that does not abide to any one place. We also balance strong effort with ease so that effort is not a goal-directed tension. We have faith and confidence in the practice, and we practice without a gaining idea.

There are various seated positions one may take in *zuo Chan*. Typically, we take a seat on a cushion, also known as *zafu* in Japanese, which sits on a mat or *zabutan*. The cross-legged position has two forms: either the full lotus or the half lotus. For the full lotus posture, cross the right leg over the left leg, and then the left leg over the right leg. For the half lotus posture, cross the right leg over the left leg, or vice versa. You can begin sitting in half lotus with the right leg and then alternate which leg you cross for each meditation session. You will gradually train both legs to sit in half lotus, and eventually, the legs may extend enough so that you can begin sitting in full lotus, first in daily meditation, and then during long retreats.

If either lotus position is not possible, the Burmese position is another option. To achieve this, place the left foot next to the inner right thigh, and the right foot next to and outside the left knee.

The Japanese *seizan* position does not require crossing the legs. For this position, place the cushion between the legs before sitting with the knees on the mat in parallel position. Some people use a meditation bench instead of a cushion for this position. Finally, it is also possible to use an ergonomic meditation chair or a regular chair.

The important element in any of these seated positions is to maintain a balance of tension, extension, and distension. If we do not extend the muscles beyond what they are capable, then we will get very relaxed and fall asleep. If we extend the muscles too much, then we will be too tense and will not be able to maintain the posture through the length of time of the meditation period. If you can sit in full lotus, it is best to sit in full lotus; otherwise, sit in half lotus, in the Burmese position, in *seizan*, or in a chair.

In general, try to keep the same posture, without moving, from the beginning to the end of the period. Move if you need to, but, if possible, remain still. When each person finds the optimal balance that is right for them, between extension, tension, and distension, then all the positions are equal and represent the living, sitting, breathing body of Buddha.

All these positions and possibilities have the common purpose of establishing the breath. To do this, first, we sit upright and with the head resting on top of the spine as if pulled by a string from the crown of the head and toward the heavens. Whether thinking or praying, our prayers, thoughts, and feelings ascend to the heavens through this upward string. There is an exchange of energy and heat between the body and the universe through the crown of the head. It flows from the universe to the body, and from the body (starting from the knees and feet, and rising to the navel, spine, and head) to the universe. We keep our back straight by pushing the lower back forward. At the same time, we keep the head straight by tucking the chin slightly inwards and keeping the eyes slightly open in a 30-degree angle toward the floor. The tongue is held in relaxed posture against the roof of the mouth. We do not grind the teeth, and the muscles in the face are relaxed.

Second, before assuming the mudra posture for the hands, rest the hands, palms facing up, on each knee, to establish the breathing practice. Inhale through the nose, and exhale through the mouth with the mouth slightly open. With each inhale through the nose, expand the stomach. And with each exhale through the mouth, contract the stomach. At the end of an exhale, inwardly count one. Cycle the breath like this three times. After taking three breaths, assume the mudra hand posture, and from then on, exhale through the nose. Count one number at the end of each exhale (one for the first exhale, two for the second exhale, etc.) until you reach ten, and start over at one. It is also possible to count to five or count one each time we exhale.

Third, after establishing the breathing practice, the hands are held in the mudra posture. The left hand rests on the right hand, with thumb tips slightly touching. The mudra is the barometer of the posture. If the body is too relaxed, or starts to fall asleep, the thumbs will start falling downward on each other. If the body is too tense, then the thumbs will start leaning upward, turning the mudra into a triangle instead of a circle. Gently touching thumbs held in a horizontal line represents the optimal balance between tension and distension and a form of connection without clinging attachment.

Fourth, after body posture and breathing have been established, the practice of mind begins. As we observe the mind as a posture within the posture, thoughts, feelings and sensations will continuously arise. It is important not to be disturbed by them, and let them arrive or arise, and then fall and leave. Try to avoid suppressing or repressing thoughts or feelings. But also try not to hold on to them by clinging, reflection, association, or analysis, or by working ourselves into a frenzy or a state of agitation. Some people recommend becoming conscious of them before letting them go. The moment of letting go can coincide with the moment of returning to the breath. We will be constantly distracted from awareness of breathing and return to awareness of breathing. In the process, we experience the impermanence of mental phenomena, as the content of our thinking, and the quality of our feelings, constantly change. Just as we try not to avoid unpleasant feelings, try also not cling to pleasant or mystical feelings. Simply let things be what they are, beyond good and bad, sacred or profane.

If physical discomfort arises, try to avoid feeding them into becoming emotional suffering. Instead, bring your awareness back to your posture, breathing, and relaxed balance of tension, extension, and distension. The more open the body is, the more room there is for accepting pain, rather than rejecting it and becoming tense and emotionally upset. If we can accept the sensation of pain, there is the possibility of experiencing how the sensation changes and turns into something else. This in turn cultivates equanimity in pain or pleasure, thinking or not thinking, success or failure in practice.

In Chan practice, the forms that we observe in the *Chantang*, *zendo*, or meditation hall are continuous with the practice of sitting cross-legged in the lotus posture. However, for the newcomer, this is not always obvious. At first, the way of walking in the *Chantang*, how we hold the hands, or how we bow may seem extremely formal or rigid. In fact, this is how we hold the emptiness of the mind in the forms of the body. But if we have ideas about correct or incorrect forms, doing it well or doing it wrong, then these can become forms of tainted, rigid, or stinking Chan. Until we know and understand how to practice, making mistakes is not only not a problem, but it is an opportunity to practice. In the beginning, we try to avoid constant correction and fixating on all the details of the forms of sitting, breathing, etc. Instead, we allow people the space and time to discover the forms on their own and by observation and experience.

Bibliography

Aitken, R. (1990). *The Gateless Barrier. The Wu-Men Kuan (Mumonkan)*. San Francisco: North Point Press.

Anacker, S. (1984a). *Seven Works of Vasubandhu: The Buddhist Psychological Doctor*. New Delhi: Motilal Banarsidass.

Anacker, S. (1984b). "The Teaching of the Three Own-beings". In: *Seven Works of Vasubhandu. The Buddhist Psychological Doctor*. New Delhi: Motilal Banarsidass.

Batchelor, S. (2000). *Verses from the Center*. New York: Riverhead Books.

Braunstein, N. (2014). *El Goce: Un Concepto Lacaniano*. Mexico: Siglo XXI.

Cleary, T. (2005). *Book of Serenity. One Hundred Zen Dialogues*. Trans. Thomas Cleary. Boston.

Coward, H. & Foshay, T. (1992). *Derrida and Negative Theology*. New York: State University of New York Press.

de la Valle, Poussin, L. (1932–1933). *Le petit traite de Vasubandhu-Nagarjuna sur le trois natures*. In: *Melanges Chinois et Bouddhiques*, II, pp. 147–161.

Demiéville, P. (1954). *"La Yogācārabhūmi de Sangharaksa"* ("The *Yogācārabhūmi* of *Sangharaksa*"). Bulletin du *l'École française d'Extrême-Orient*, 2, 44, 2: 339–436.

Derrida, J. (1978). *Writing and Difference*. Trans. Alan Bass. Chicago: University of Chicago Press.

Dirac, P. (1928). The Quantum Theory of the Electron. https://royalsocietypublishing.org/doi/10.1098/rspa.1928.0023. Accessed April 22, 2020.

Dogen, E. (1200/1997) *Shobogenzo: The True Dharma-Eye Treasure*. London and Tokyo.

Dogen, E. (1241a [1998]). *Kokyo*. In: *Shobogenzo*. London and Tokyo: Windmill Publications.

Dogen, E. (1241b [1998]). *Bussho*. In: *Shobogenzo*. London and Tokyo: Windmill Publications.

Ferguson, A. (2000). *Zen's Chinese Heritage: The Masters and Their Teachings*. Boston: Wisdom Publications. Kindle Edition.

Feuerbach, L. (1841 [1957]). *The Essence of Christianity*. London: Kegan Paul, Trench, Trübner & Co.; New York: Harper & Row (Harper Torchbooks).

Fink, B. (1995). *The Lacanian Subject. Between Language and Jouissance*. New Jersey: Princeton University Press.

Freud, S. (1895). *A Project for a Scientific Psychology*. SE 1, 283–397.

Freud, S. (1900a). *The Interpretation of Dreams*, G.W., II–III, 503; S.E., V, 499.

Freud, S. (1900b [1965]). *The Interpretation of Dreams*. New York: Avon Books.

Freud, S. (1913). *Totem and Taboo*. SE, 13: 1–161.

Freud, S. (1914). *The Moses of Michelangelo*. SE, 13: 211–238.

Freud, S. (1915). *Instincts and their Vicissitudes*. SE, 14: 111–140

Freud, S. (1920 [1961]). *Beyond the Pleasure Principle*. New York: Norton & Norton. SE 18: 7–64.

Freud, S. (1924). *The Economic Problem of Masochism*. SE, 19, 157–170.

Han, S. (2018). Poetics of Mu. *Textual Practice*, 34, 6: 921–948, DOI: 10.1080/0950236X.2018.1515790

Han, S. (2022). *□: To Regard a Wave*. Chicago, IL: Selva Oscura Press.

Heidegger, M. (1966). *Discourse on Thinking*. Trans. John M. Anderson and E. Hans Freund. New York: Harper and Row.

Heine, S. (2012). Four Myths about Zen Buddhism's Mu Koan. https://blog.oup.com/2012/04/four-myths-about-zen-buddhisms-mu-koan. Accessed March 29, 2020.

Hofstadter, D.R. (1979 [1999]). *Gödel, Escher, Bach: an Eternal Golden Braid*. New York: Basic Books.

Kim, H.J. (2004). *Eihei Dogen: Mystical Realist*. Boston: Wisdom Publications.

Kochumuttom, T.A. (1982). *A Buddhist Doctrine of Experience*. New Delhi: Motilal Banarsidass.

Lacan, J. (1953–1954 [1991]). *The Seminar of Jacques Lacan. Book I Freud's Papers on Technique*. New York: Norton.

Lacan, J. (1954–1955 [1991]). *The Seminar of Jacques Lacan. Book II the Ego in Freud's Theory and in the Technique of Psychoanalysis*. New York: Norton.

Lacan, J. (1955–1956 [1977]). *Seminar III on Psychoses. The Seminar of Jacques Lacan, Book III: The Psychoses*. New York: Norton.

Lacan, J. (1959–1960 [2010]). *The Seminar of Jacques Lacan, Book VII: The Ethics of Psychoanalysis*. London: Routledge.

Lacan, J. (1960 [2013]). *The Triumph of Religion*. Cambridge: Polity Press.

Lacan, J. (1960–1961 [2017]). *Transference: The Seminar of Jacques Lacan. Book VIII*. London: Polity Press.

Lacan, J. (1962–1963). *The Seminar of Jacques Lacan. Book X Anxiety*. Trans. Cormac Gallagher from unedited French typescripts. www.lacaninireland.com/web/wp-content/uploads/2010/06/Seminar-X-Revised-by-Mary-Cherou-Lagreze.pdf. Accessed March 28, 2020.

Lacan, J. (1962–1963 [2014]). *The Seminar of Jacques Lacan. Book X Anxiety*. Ed. J.-A. Miller, Trans. A. Price. Cambridge: Polity.

Lacan, J. (1964 [1981]). *The Four Fundamental Concepts of Psychoanalysis*. New York: Norton.

Lacan, J. (1966a [2006]). "The Function and Field of Language and Speech in Psychoanalysis". In: *Ecrits*. Trans. B. Fink. New York and London: Norton.

Lacan, J. (1966b [2006]). "The Subversion of the Subject and the Dialectic of Desire in the Freudian Unconscious". In: *Ecrits*. Trans. B. Fink. New York and London: Norton.

Lacan, J. (1971–1972 [2018]). *Or Worse. The Seminar. Book XIX*. London: Polity Press.

Lacan, J. (1972–1973). *The Seminar of Jacques Lacan: Book XX. On Feminine Sexuality, the Limits of Love and Knowledge (Encore)*. New York: Norton and Norton.

Lacan, J. (1973 [1991]). *Télévision*. Paris: Seuil [*Television: A Challenge to the Psychoanalytic Establishment*, Ed. Joan Copjec, Trans. Denis Hollier, Rosalind Krauss and Annette Michelson. New York: Norton.

Lacan, J. (1975). *La Troisième Jouissance. Lettres de l'ecole freudienne*, 16: 178–203.

Lacan, J. (1975–1976). *Joyce and the Sinthome. Seminar XXIII*. Trans. Cormac Gallagher. Unpublished. Lacaninireland.com. Accessed March 29, 2020.

Lacan, J. (1975–1976 [2018]). *The Sinthome: The Seminar of Jacques Lacan, Book XXIII*. Ed. J.A. Miller. Cambridge: Polity Press.

Lacan, J. (2005). *De los Nombres del Padre*. Buenos Aires: Paidos.

Leader, D. (2021). *Jouissance. Sexuality, Suffering, and Satisfaction*. Cambridge: Polity Press.

Levi-Strauss, C. (1949). *The Elementary Structures of Kinship*. Boston: Beacon Press, 1969.

Loy, D. (1992). "The Deconstruction of Buddhism". In: *Derrida and Negative Theology*. New York: State University of New York Press.

Maddox, B. (1988). Joyce, Nora and the Word Known to All Men. *The. New York Times*, May 15, 1998. www.nytimes.com/1988/05/15/books/joyce-nora-and-the-word-known-to-all-men.html

Merton, T. (1965). *The Way of Chuang Tzu*. New York: New Directions.

Moncayo, R. (2008). *Evolving Lacanian Perspective for Clinical Psychoanalysis*. London: Karnac.

Moncayo, R. (1997). "Freud's Concepts of Drive, Desire, and Nirvana" in *Umbra (a): A journal of the Unconscious. #1 on the drive*. 121–130.

Moncayo, R. (2012). *The Signifier Pointing at the Moon: Psychoanalysis and Zen Buddhism*. London: Karnac.

Moncayo, R. (2018). *Knowing, Not-Knowing, and Jouissance. Levels, Symbols, and Jouisssance*. London: Palgrave Macmillan.

Moncayo, R. (1997) "Freud's Concepts of Drive, Desire, and Nirvana" in *Umbra (a): A journal of the Unconscious. #1 on the drive*. 121–130.

Nagarjuna (100 CE [1984]). *Nagarjuna's Seventy Stanzas: A Buddhist Psychology of Emptiness*. New York: Snow Lion Publications.

Nagarjuna (100 CE [2008]). *The Root Stanzas of the Middle Way: The Mulamadhyamakakarika*. Boulder: Shambala.

Plotinus (204–70 CE [1991]). *The Enneads (Classics)*. London: Penguin Books. Kindle Edition.

Ricoeur, P. (1970). *Freud and Philosophy*. New Haven: Yale University Press.

Roudinesco, E. (1997 [1993]). *Jacques Lacan*. Trans. B. Bray. New York, NY and London: Columbia University Press.

Safran, J. (2003). *Psychoanalysis and Buddhism: An Unfolding Dialogue*. Boston: Wisdom Publication.

Suzuki, S. (1974). *Zen Mind Beginner's Mind*. New York: Weatherhill.

West, J. (2013). Torricelli and the Ocean of Air: The First Measurement of Barometric Pressure. *Physiology (Bethesda)*, March, 28, 2: 66–73.

Yun, X. Chan Heart, Chan Art. https://terebess.hu/zen/mesterek/ChanHeart-Chinese.pdf. Accessed June 30, 2022.

Index

Dirac, Paul 38
discriminating knowledge (*connaissance*)
32, 50
Dogen Zenji xii, 31, 33, 36, 54–55, 56–57,
59, 73; *see also* Mirror
Dongshan (Dongshan Liangjie) 29,
41, 54
dreams: analysand's as clinical example
83–85; of anxiety or punishment 22

"Economic Problem of Masochism, The"
(Freud) 24
Ecrits (Lacan) 20
ego: ego ideal 20, 51; ego-Id formations
21; egoism contrasted with altruism
2; ideal ego and drive 20; in Joyce's
writing 51–52; repression and the
pleasure principle 18–20; vanishing
under signifier 26; *see also* Symbolic,
the
Einstein, Albert, and constancy principle
15–16
emptiness: affirmation or denial 55; as
bridge 7; and energy waves 38; as form
of jouissance 35, 76–77; and Other
36; of presence and of absence 12; and
productivity 29; and understanding 19;
see also Wu
energy: dark energy 15; kinetic energy 23;
quiescent energy 23, 25
enlightenment x, 34, 54, 55; *see also* light
ex-sistence 17, 18, 47–48
Eye and Treasury of the True Law, The 59
eyes: Buddha's half-shut eyes 81; in
dreams 84; fabricated eyes and mirrors
71–72; *Kuan-yin*'s eyes 81; as mirror
58–59, 65

fantasy xi, 12; *see also* Imaginary, the;
objet a
Fechner, Gustav Theodor 14
femininity 64; feminine sexuality 80;
see also "woman"
Feuerbach, Ludwig 35
fictions, and emptiness 12
Fink, B. 40
Finnegans Wake (Joyce) 48–49
free association vii, 10, 36, 44, 47
Frege, Gottlob 50
Freud, Sigmund: altruism and egoism 2;
on Nirvana 6, 9–13; Pcpt.-Cs. system
19–20; photograph of 66; pleasure
principle 15, 23–24; reality principle 3;

repetition compulsion 21; use of term
Nirvana 39
"Function and Field of Speech and
Language in Psychoanalysis, The" 46

Gateless Barrier 29
*Gödel, Escher, Bach: an Eternal Golden
Braid* (Hofstadter) 43, 46
Gödel, Kurt 15; Gödel's theorem 43, 46,
49–50, 77
Gong'an; *see* koans
ground zero states 17
Guanyin (Guanshiyin) 1

Han, Sora viii
"Han" xii–xiii
hedonism 20
Heidegger, Martin vii, 7–8
Helmholtz, Hermann von 23
Hilbert, David 50
Hinayana Buddhism 7
Hinduism 29, 40–41
Hofstadter, Douglas R. 43–44, 46,
49–50
holes: Freudian unconscious as false 24;
Real unconscious as 16, 17; within
the Symbolic 48, 51; symbolic hole,
Nomination process 4–5
homeostasis, and pleasure principle 26
human beings (Ren), definitions 2

Imaginary, the: as aspect of self-nature
3; in Chan Mirror of Mind 62; in knot
of four 2; in knot of three 4; in RSI
framework 47–48
imaginary knowledge (*connaissance*)
32, 50
imaginary numbers 38
incest 22
inertia 14
"Instance of the Letter, The" (Lacan) 44

Joshu's dog 30, 43–44
jouissance: analyst/analysand 32;
contrasted with Symbolic 4; emptiness
as form of 76–77; as energetic default
state 38; feminine as Third jouissance
80; and Joyce's *Finnegans Wake* 49; and
moments of insight 70; Other jouissance
19, 40; overview and definitions 3, 7;
phallic jouissance xi, 64–65; pleasure
and suffering 26; and the Real 52; Third
jouissance 5, 8, 34–35, 60, 65; three

non-thinking 5
no-self 40, 41
not-having 33; *see also* Wu
no-thing 5, 8, 34, 36, 65, 76
not-thinking 9–10

objet a 6, 19, 28, 30, 33, 62–64, 65
objetality 73
"On Drives and their Vicissitudes"
    (Freud) 2
One, the: and Buddha 77; control of
    subject 69; Imaginary One with mother
    xii; master as 21
orgasm 9
Osaku-sendaba 36
Other, the: Clear Mirror as 65, 68; and
    desire 28, 35–36; European and
    Asian Othering of each other xii–xiii;
    jouissance of 12, 19; Lacan's symbolic
    Other 3; the Other-Dependent 3; as
    represented by signifier 40; speech of
    neurotic 47

Padmapani; see Avalokiteśvara
pantheism/panentheism 74–75
Pascal, Blaise 37
Pcpt.-Cs. system 24, 29, 60, 70
phallus: phallic jouissance xi, 12, 80;
    symbolism of 35, 64–65, 84–85
physics 15; *see also* science
placenta 35
Plato 63
pleasure principle 10–11, 15, 18–20,
    22–26
practice-enlightenment 34
Psyche and Mind 9
psychoanalysis: analyst, presence of
    20–21; analytic process 9–10; clinical
    dream example 83–85; contrasted with
    traditional culture 36; and the cultural
    Other xiii; and Death 26; as depth
    psychology 69; epiphanies during 70;
    and experience of "Just This" 76; and
    free association 10, 36, 44, 47; and
    non-assertion 55; paradoxes between
    language and speech 46–47; paradox
    of the subject 47; payment for 79; as
    science 20–21; signifier shifting 62;
    transference love 82
Psychoanalysis and Buddhism (Safran) vii
psychosis 4, 47
punishment dreams 22–23

quantum mechanics 38
quietism 12

Real, the: as aspect of self-nature
    3; contrasted with Imaginary 12;
    contrasted with reality 3–4; Freud's
    reality principle 3–4; and hole created
    by Symbolic 4–5, 17; and jouissance
    3, 52; Lacan's definitions 3–5; and
    Other jouissance 40; Real of thought
    74; in RSI framework 47–48; subject
    of the sinthome 51; Truth as form of
    jouissance 34–35
reality principle 18–19, 20
Real Unconsciousness 16, 17, 24, 70
recognition, desire for 24, 59
recycling, metaphor for analytic process 82
relativity, theory of 38
repetition compulsion 6, 18, 21–22, 27
Repressed Unconsciousness 17–19, 20, 22,
    48, 49, 70
repression 20, 24
Ricoeur, P. 25–26
riddles and signifiers 8
Rimbaud, Arthur 40
Rinzai zen 12, 29, 30–31, 34, 39; *see also*
    Linchi (Línjì) school
"Rome Report" (Lacan) 46
Roudinesco, E. vii
RSI (Real-Symbolic-Imaginary)
    framework 3, 47–48
Russell, Bertrand 50

Safran, J. vii
Samsāra xii, 6, 21
savoir (symbolic knowledge) 21, 29, 32,
    39, 50
science: negative consequences of
    74; paradox of subject in scientific
    discourse 47; vacuum in Western
    science 37–38
Self, higher 40, 41
self-nature, threefold aspect of 3
self-referentiality, Gödelian 50, 51
Seminar on the Names of the Father 35
Seminar VIII 63–64
Seminar X (on Anxiety) vii, ix, 5, 58, 84
Seminar XI x
Seminar XIX 5
Seminar XX 80
Seminar XXI 8
Seminar XXII 3

For Product Safety Concerns and Information please contact our EU
representative GPSR@taylorandfrancis.com
Taylor & Francis Verlag GmbH, Kaufingerstraße 24, 80331 München, Germany

9 781032 056975